35938
"White Winter Pearmain"
L. S. Zinny,
E. U. Farnham Watsonville Cal.
Jersey City N. J.
Lot 163 Ripe,
4-10-'06   Stored immediately   A. A. Newton
4-13-06

Amanda Almira Newton, *Malus domestica*, White Winter Pearmain, 1906.

The GHOST ORCHARD

ALSO BY HELEN HUMPHREYS

The GHOST ORCHARD

THE HIDDEN HISTORY OF
THE APPLE IN NORTH AMERICA

HELEN HUMPHREYS

HarperCollins*Publishers*Ltd

Published by HarperCollins Publishers Ltd

First edition

HarperCollins Publishers Ltd
2 Bloor Street East, 20th Floor
Toronto, Ontario, Canada
M4W 1A8

www.harpercollins.ca

Library and Archives Canada Cataloguing in Publication information
is available upon request.

ISBN 978-1-44345-151-2

Printed and bound in the United States

LSC/H 9 8 7 6 5 4 3 2 1

In loving memory of Joanne Page

When eating a fruit, think of the person who planted the tree.

—VIETNAMESE PROVERB

Each autumn a dozen little red apples hung on one of its branches like a line of poetry in a foreign language.

—EDWARD THOMAS

CONTENTS

The GHOST ORCHARD

Last fall I was eating wild apples, and a close friend of mine was slowly dying. I was thinking a lot about death and friendship, and overtop of that was the sweet, dense taste of the White Winter Pearmain: the crisp of its flesh, a juicy surprise, each time I bit into it.

The apple tree stood beside a log cabin. The tree is dead now, killed by the harsh winter, its lace of dry branches a filigree through which I can see the green spring trees plumping the field edge when I come here to walk the dog.

The cabin is long deserted, its windows smashed out by weekend partiers and the loft now inhabited by a colony of raccoons. The teenagers and the raccoons have treated the house in much the same way—destroying the walls and shitting in the corners. The raccoons upstairs, the teenagers down. When I drove out there tonight, the raccoons tried to warn me away from the building with a chorus of yelps.

But I'm not interested in the house. It's the tree I came for.

Just last year, when the tree was still alive, I ate its apples all autumn. They were yellow-skinned, with a faint pink blush on one side where the sun had touched them. They were late apples, ripening in October and still edible into December. They also had an extraordinary taste—crisp and juicy with an underlay of pear and honey.

The tree was mature but not ancient, the last holdout from an old orchard, perhaps, or planted by the former owner of the property. There had probably once been other apple trees nearby—earlier-blooming ones so that the fruit could be eaten and cooked from late summer until Christmas. A late apple will sometimes keep in storage right through winter.

The White Winter Pearmain is thought to have come from Rome, but it was first documented in Norfolk, England, in AD 1200. From there it moved to America in the late eighteenth century, and while it is not a popular heritage apple today, it is still being grown and is prized for its late fruiting and for its taste. Because the apple has a hint of pear—hence the "pearmain"[1] in its name—it has a complex flavour, and it is this complexity, this overlapping of apple and pear in the same fruit, that has led to it being called the best-tasting apple in the world.

When I was growing up on the outskirts of Toronto, there were rogue apple trees in all the nearby fields. We climbed them and made forts in them and pelted other children with the hard unripe fruit. The scent in autumn in the fields was the scent of rotting apples and the sound was the buzz of wasps over the soft, sticky pulp on the ground. There was a particularly old apple tree up the street from my house. Its low branches made it easy to climb, and my friends and I hauled up wood and nails and made a series of platforms in the tree, using an old tire and a rope as a makeshift elevator to move us and the building supplies up and down. In my melancholic teenage years, I would sit in the branches among the apples, thinking my gloomy thoughts and listening to the wind rustle the leaves around my perch.

Back then, I took the fact of the apple trees at the edge of our neighbourhood for granted. Now, I realize that the immense size of that one tree I used to climb probably meant it was at least a century old—which is ancient for an apple tree. I wish I had been interested enough at the time to think of investigating what variety of apple tree it was, because all the varieties have a story attached to them, and because, in the nineteenth-century heyday of apples, there were upwards of seventeen thousand different varieties in North American orchards.[2] Today there are fewer than a hundred varieties grown commercially, and often less than a dozen varieties for sale in our grocery stores. When we think of apples, we tend to think of Granny Smith, Gala, Red Delicious,

Honeycrisp, and perhaps something with a little more exoticism, like Ginger Gold or Orange Pippin. When we think of tales about apples, we think primarily of the over-mythologized Johnny Appleseed.

This is what the seventeen thousand different varieties have been reduced to.

There must be more to the story of the apple than the history that is so readily available. There must be a way to describe—simply and beautifully—the taste of an apple.

The presence of death brings life into sharper focus, makes some things more important and others less so. I couldn't stop my friend's death, or fight against it. I stood out by the log cabin and the dead tree that night and thought that what I could do was make a journey alongside Joanne—a journey that was about something life-affirming, something as basic and fundamental as an apple. I could take my curiosity about the White Winter Pearmain and use it as a portal to examine the lost history of some of the lost apples.

The INDIAN ORCHARD

What makes apples so interesting is that like human beings, they are individuals, and their history has paralleled our history.

The apple is a member of the rose family. It originated some 4.5 million years ago in Kazakhstan, where, until the latter part of the twentieth century, there were still large forests of apple trees growing wild in the countryside.[1] The fruit made its way to Europe via trade routes and was brought from Europe to North America by settlers in the seventeenth century.

Apples are not indigenous to North America.

They were brought over by the European settlers who arrived on the continent in the early 1600s. An orchard was essential to the survival of the incomers because apples were hearty and could provide sustenance throughout the long winter months. In fact, at the beginning of the 1800s, America enacted a law saying that homesteaders had to plant an orchard of at least fifty apple trees during their first year of settlement.[2] This law gave rise to many plant nurseries, established to furnish the settlers with the young trees they needed.

The recorded history of the apple in North America is the history of white settlement during the nineteenth century. It is the history of plant nurseries and cider orchards and fruit catalogues, as well as the slightly mad figure of Johnny Appleseed (John Chapman), traversing the countryside with his sack of seeds, planting trees for cider orchards and opening seedling nurseries to supply the settlers with young trees, called whips, so they could grow their own.

Apples can be propagated from seed, but the resulting tree will probably not resemble the tree from which the seed was taken. This is because each blossom on an apple tree is likely being visited by a different pollinator. So the bee that pollinates blossom A doesn't necessarily visit blossom B, and that bee also carries on its body pollen from other apple trees it has visited. As a result, the mix in each individual apple is different and distinct, so the seeds of each apple on any given tree will be 50 percent from the tree of origin and 50 percent from another apple tree, perhaps even one of a different type. The only way to keep apples uniform is to graft on to a rootstock, and this is the method by which all apples are commercially grown. It was also the method used by early European growers and by North American settlers to produce reliable apple varieties.

When apples are planted from seed, without grafting, no two trees will be exactly alike and often the fruit will be inedible "spitters." But even an apple that's no good for eating is usually fine for drinking, and orchards of ungrafted apples were often used as cider orchards. John Chapman, in giving and selling ungrafted apple seedlings, was supplying settlers with the makings for cider orchards, and much of colonial American life was probably experienced through a heavy alcoholic haze (which, quite frankly, might have made it more bearable).

Johnny Appleseed wasn't the only one planting seeds. Most of the indigenous peoples were also cultivating apple orchards. In fact, "Indian orchard" was a common term, described in nineteenth-century dictionaries as "an old orchard of ungrafted apple-trees, the time of planting being unknown."[3] So-called Indian orchards were once literally everywhere in what is now the United States. In 1889 in Ohio, a Colonel Howard wrote in a letter to the Ohio State Board of Agriculture that when he was a boy, he had eaten apples that grew from trees on "Indian Island" and on the left bank of the Maumee River, and that many of the trees were at least a century old. He had also eaten apples from an old Indian orchard in the village of Nawash, and he planned a return trip there as an old man, to eat apples "from trees from which I picked fruit nearly three-quarters of a century ago."[4]

There was a Tuscarora orchard in Oneida County, in the middle of New York State, that was planted around 1715 and was described as having several hundred apple trees in it.[5] There was a Seneca orchard in the hamlet of Egypt in Ontario County, New York.[6] The Algonquians had many orchards in Southern Ontario.[7] The Cherokee orchards in the southern United States were so plentiful that a nurseryman named Jarvis Van Buren collected seedling apples from them in the 1850s to use for sale.[8] The first commercial orchard in the United States was rumoured to have been started in Maysville, Arkansas, by a Cherokee woman who used African American slaves to do her labour. When the slaves were liberated after the Civil War, she was unable to work the land anymore. The orchard was subsequently purchased by a white settler, H. S. Mundell, who continued to operate it commercially.[9]

When the incomers were looking for a place to settle in the eighteenth and nineteenth centuries, land with an already thriving orchard was enticing. It is no accident that many of the white settlements sprang up where there was an indigenous orchard. But first, of course, the original owners had to be vanquished. The apple thus became, in its infancy in North America, a tool for colonialism.

In Lafayette, New York, the first white settlement was made at Haskin's Hill, a little to the east of an Indian orchard, by a John Wilcox in 1791. Wilcox commandeered the orchard and sold the fruit to other early settlers. The orchard was over twenty acres in size, and its trees were planted in regular rows and were very productive.[10]

There was an Indian orchard in White Mills, Pennsylvania, and another in Buffalo, New York. Guilford, New York, was once the site of an Oneida apple orchard. Apple Creek, Missouri, was built on the site of Shawnee orchards. In Michigan's Saginaw valley, there were apparently Indian orchards as early as 1750.[11] Apple trees recorded by white settlers in 1824 were already at least sixty years old at the time of discovery, and they were "generally conceded to have been from seeds of fruit brought by the Indians from Canada on their returns from their annual trips to receive annuities from the British government at [Fort] Malden, Ontario."[12]

The Indian orchard in Terre Haute, Indiana, dated from the early 1700s and was the site of a Wea legend. The legend concerned a young white woman named Lena, who for years had lived with a Delaware community on the banks of the Wabash River. She had been captured as a child and grew up as a member of the tribe, happy in her new family. In 1763, the Pennsylvania government wanted to forge an alliance with the tribes along the Ohio and Wabash Rivers; part of the agreement was that the Shawnees would try to return captured whites to their original families. A Shawnee brave named Nemo was dispatched to collect the captives from the Delaware village where Lena lived. She was reluctant to leave with him, but her Delaware father saw the futility of fighting the Shawnees, as well as the white government of Pennsylvania, and persuaded Lena to go.

The two travelled for weeks together, and in that time they talked and shared their feelings and fell in love. By the time they'd reached the Shawnee village where Nemo lived, they had decided that they wanted to marry and remain together. But it was illegal in the 1700s for whites and Native Americans to marry, and so, one night when everyone was sleeping, Nemo and Lena left the village to return to Lena's Delaware home along the banks of the Wabash, where they would set up a life together.

The journey was arduous and included an encounter with three Miami braves, whom Nemo killed and scalped. When he and Lena arrived at the Delaware village, however, there was nothing left but the smoking ruins of the wigwams. There had been a fight within the community; Lena's family had been killed, and those who remained had moved on. Undeterred, the couple built a wigwam and had a child. Lena planted some apple seeds, and a fledgling orchard appeared.

But the happiness of the couple was short-lived: a band of Miami warriors found their encampment and killed Nemo after a long and valiant struggle. Lena, in her despair, handed her infant son to one

19258
Buff
C.R. McGuiry
Paint Gap Yancey Co. N.C
3-9-1900
J.G.Passmore

Deborah Griscom Passmore, *Malus domestica*, Buff, 1900.

32668
Seneca Favorite
O. M. Taylor. Geneva Exp. Sta.
Geneva, Ontario, N.Y.

D. G. Passmore
10.22.1904

Deborah Griscom Passmore, *Malus domestica*, Seneca Favorite, 1904.

No. 32735
Indian Favorite ~~Grower~~
Mr. Wm Beck.
Union Co., Indiana.

E. I. Schutt
Oct 24 1904

Ellen Isham Schutt, *Malus domestica*, Indian Favorite, 1904.

Royal Charles Steadman, *Malus domestica*, Nickajack, 1923.

of the Miami braves and plunged Nemo's scalping knife into her heart, to join him in death.

According to the legend, Nemo and Lena's son grew up to be a warrior and fought alongside Tecumseh. The grave of the two lovers became a sacred place. In the spring, Shawnee maidens who crossed the orchard—for the trees had grown into a beautiful apple orchard—would place wildflowers on the grave, and all agreed to leave the trees alone so that the spirits of Nemo and Lena could use the apples as nourishment. The grave and the orchard became consecrated ground to the people along the Wabash. When the white settlers took possession of the orchard in the 1830s, they buried their dead there and called it Old Indian Orchard Cemetery.

One of the largest indigenous orchards was in what is now Geneva, New York. It was previously a Seneca village called Kanadesaga and was known as the "castle" of the Seneca—essentially their capital. There were extensive apple and peach orchards, as well as plum, mulberry, hickory, walnut and butternut trees. Squash and corn were also grown in profusion.[13] And there was a Seneca burial mound near the village.

In 1779, Major General John Sullivan, with an army of some four thousand men, was sent by President George Washington to destroy the Six Nations and determine "at a single blow, whether white men or red men should hold domination over these fertile vales and along these streams, and over these lakes and mountains."[14] Sullivan and his men started out in June and made their way through the Finger Lakes region of New York State, burning out and destroying forty villages and towns belonging to the Iroquois nation.[15]

Before reaching Geneva, Sullivan's army arrived at the small indigenous town of Chonodote, known as Peach Orchard, which was located near Cayuga and had "not less than 1,500 [peach] trees, thrifty, and loaded with fruit."[16] The soldiers set fire to the town and orchard, an act of destruction described by one as "the monotonous work of ruin."[17]

Kendaia, also on the edge of Seneca Lake and known to the white settlers as Appletown, was destroyed as well. It was described by one of Sullivan's officers, a Major John Burrowes, as having "the best houses I have seen and about 15 of them, with an orchard of seventy trees, to appearance had been planted fifty years."[18] The inhabitants of the town had fled two days in advance of the arrival of Sullivan's troops.

The men arrived in Geneva on September 7, 1779. The wealth of the Seneca agricultural system was described by Reverend David Craft in an address about the expedition to President Washington:

Kanadesaga was a large and important town, consisting of fifty houses with thirty more in the immediate vicinity, and being the [capital] of the nation was frequently called the "Seneca Castle." Its site was on the present Castle road, a mile and a half west from Geneva. The town was divided by Kanadesaga or Castle Creek . . . Orchards of apple, peach and mulberry trees surrounded the town. Fine gardens with onions, peas, beans, squashes, potatoes, turnips, cabbages, cucumbers, water melons, carrots and parsnips abounded: and large cornfields were to the north and northeast of the town. All were destroyed on the 7th of September.[19]

Sullivan's army eliminated the Seneca food source by girdling the apple orchards and burning the crops.

To "girdle" a tree is to cut a width of bark from its circumference, thus preventing the sap from rising to the branches. It is an effective way to kill a tree— and a cruel one, as the tree still looks alive, in that it is standing and any blossoms or fruit or leaves on it at the time of the girdling remain. It was favoured as a method of destruction by armies because it requires a lot less effort than cutting down a tree, saving the strength and energy of the men.

I have tried myself, mostly to failed effect, to grow a small orchard on a river property I have in Eastern Ontario. The winter before last was so cold that mice, tunnelling below the layer of thick ice that covered the ground, ate the bark around the base of my apple trees, girdling them. I was able to save one tree by wrapping duct tape around the damaged area; the tape acted as a substitute skin and allowed the sap to move from the roots to the branches. But the other trees died, and the frustration and dismay I felt at the sight of these otherwise healthy trees stopped by something so small as a mouse would have been, I imagine, but a fraction of what the Senecas felt at the killing of their orchards by Sullivan's army. In early September, the apples would have been on the trees and almost ripe.

With the destruction of their land and gardens and orchards, the Senecas had no choice but to flee to Fort Niagara to appeal for protection and food from the British soldiers who were stationed there, and who had been their allies against the Americans in the Revolutionary War a few years earlier. The British tried to assist the refugees, but they simply didn't have enough food to give the approximately five thousand people, two-thirds of them women, children and elders.[20] The winter of 1779 was particularly cold, and many of the Seneca families starved or froze to death.

Their stolen land was, of course, valuable to the settlers, and the first white settlement started in 1787, on the site of Kanadesaga. The dead trees of the orchards must have remained, as the land was described at the time of purchase as being "covered by an Indian orchard, and the ground has never been plowed, because of a stipulation to that effect made with the Indians in the treaty of purchase. It contains an Indian burial ground . . . [and] was the largest Indian settlement in western New York."[21]

Shoots, or "sprouts" (as they were called then), from the old Seneca apple trees flourished and grew into trees that eventually bore fruit and were used by the incomers. A resident of Geneva wrote in 1799 that "the apple and peach orchards left by the Indians yield every year [an] abundance of fruit for the use of the inhabitants, besides making considerable cyder; so much so that one farmer near Geneva sold cyder this year to the amount of $1,200."[22] (This is equivalent to almost $24,000 in 2017.)

The Seneca burial mound at Kanadesaga, although protected in the initial bill of sale to the white settlers, was later built on. In the 1950s, there was a diner on the site. The owners, who in the construction discovered artifacts and skeletons of the Seneca dead, called their restaurant the Indian Mound Diner.

Interestingly, the New York State Agricultural Experiment Station, a division of Cornell University, is built directly across the road from the former site of Kanadesaga. The station has a heritage orchard of approximately seven thousand trees—the largest collection of individual apple trees in the world. It also runs an apple-breeding program in conjunction with local growers, inventing new varieties of apples and releasing them into the North American market. The latest of these varieties are the SnapDragon and the RubyFrost.

The importance of the apple to the Iroquois was documented at the beginning of the twentieth century by Arthur Caswell Parker, an archaeologist at the New York State Museum who produced an ethnobotany of the Iroquois and used the people themselves as the source for his bulletin. He performed dozens of interviews with members of the

Iroquois nation and determined that the apple was their favourite fruit. He even used their language to list the words for it (there are two different words for "apple," another word for "baked apple," and a fourth distinct word for "applesauce"), and he was the only early historian I found who wrote about Native Americans by actually consulting them.[23] But this was more than likely because Parker was himself of Iroquois descent—his father was a mixed-blood Seneca. When he retired from his job at the museum, he returned to the former home of the Senecas near Geneva, the land of his father, and died there at the age of seventy-three.

Perhaps because "castle" is an English word, it survived the removal of the Seneca people from Kanadesaga/Geneva. There is an Old Castle Road in the city, and Kanadesaga Creek was renamed Castle Creek. The Seneca apple trees used to grow near this creek, within the Seneca settlement, and since a margin of land on either side has never been built on, I decide to go there to look for evidence of the old indigenous orchards.

I travel down in the spring so that I can spot the apple trees—it is blossom season and the frothy mass of white and pink will be easily distinguishable from the green leaf of the other trees. I drive down on back roads bordering fields full of old orchards, the blossom so thick on the trees that it looks as if the branches are upholstered with it. The air is sweet with the scent.

I am using a facsimile of a map from 1845 as a guide at the original Kanadesaga site. This map was made by Lewis Henry Morgan, a nineteenth-century anthropologist and lawyer who was a champion of the Iroquois, representing them on land claims and writing an extensive ethnography of their society. This study influenced the thinking of Marx, Engels, Freud and Darwin. The Iroquois adopted Morgan into their Hawk clan in 1847.[24]

Morgan's map is fantastically detailed. The unit of measurement is paces, and the length of a pace is set at two and a half feet. So it is very easy to walk the perimeter of the old Seneca settlement, which Morgan determined to be roughly sixty-four by forty-one paces. At the time of his map-making, the corner posts of the old Seneca fort were still in place, and he was able to use these when he took his measurements.

The sprouts of the girdled Seneca orchard had, in the sixty-six years between the destructive acts of Sullivan's army and Morgan's visit to the site, grown back into full trees; "Indian Orchard Apple Trees" is marked clearly on Morgan's map.[25] Also on the map is a single tree near the northern boundary of the fort. Morgan has written beside it the words "Apple Tree still standing," which presumably means that it was one of the original trees and somehow escaped destruction by Sullivan's men. In the introduction to S. A. Beach's *The Apples of New York*, there is a photograph from 1904 captioned "Indian Apple Tree Still Standing"[26] in what looks to be the same spot.[27] The overlap of descriptive wording and the location of the tree make me think that the two trees could, in fact, be one and the same.

The land where the fort once stood is now occupied by a scrappy gas station and mini-mart. I buy gas so I have an excuse to be there.

By Castle Road, at what seems to have been the spot where Morgan drew the single surviving apple tree, stands a rusty historical marker from 1932 that says: "Site of Kanadesaga, Chief Castle of the Seneca Nation. Destroyed Sept. 7, 1779, in Gen. John Sullivan's Raid." Beside the marker are the remains of the frame for a large hanging sign that looks as if it could have once supported a billboard for the Indian Mound Diner or a sign for a former gas station on the site.

Just south of the broken pavement of the mini-mart parking lot is the burial mound, adrift on a small patch of grass between the gas station and some self-storage units next door. (The Indian Mound Diner once occupied the spot where the gas station is now.) The burial mound has two tombstones placed against each other on top of the rise. One is a large, modern grey stone that looks to have been erected fairly recently. It has the etched figure of a Seneca brave on it; his arms are crossed and he's standing in front of a fir tree at the edge of a lake. The second marker is from 1908 and is much smaller, but also very tombstone-like. The wording on both is interesting. The modern monument, which I imagine is meant as some sort of redress to the actions of Sullivan's army, says, "Burial Mound of Seneca Indians, Destroyed Sept. 7, 1779," which makes it seem as though the burial mound has been destroyed, when in fact it is the only thing left. The smaller gravestone simply says, "Burial Mound of the Seneca Indians." It was erected by a group called the Fortnightly Reading Club. This was a women's group, formed in Geneva and other American towns to serve as an educational forum, whose members met every two weeks to discuss books. They read only non-fiction.[28] From the group's archives, for the meeting when they studied "Indians," I learned that the women of the Fortnightly Reading Club had invited the last of the Seneca medicine men, Shango, to give a lecture, for which they sold tickets and raised enough money to erect the marker.[29]

My plan had been to walk beside the creek bed and look for apple trees, but I discover that the foliage along the creek is so dense it's hard to get more than twenty feet into the underbrush, and then I am so hunched over from avoiding branches and brambles that I can't look up to notice any apple blossom.

I back out and reconsider.

The creek is shallow and brown, choked with the vegetation crowding its banks and full of dead branches. Any plan to walk along it is now shelved also. I stand on the grass, in a clear spot by the road, trying to think of what to do next, and then I notice something strange. Across the creek is a low drystone wall. The stones range from the size of a fist to the size of a watermelon, and the wall runs for about fifty feet and then stops. It does not serve any purpose that I can discern; it's too short for a boundary marker and it's well back from the creek, so it wouldn't be of use as a breakwater. And the creek is barely a trickle, so it's hard to imagine that it ever floods.

Lewis Morgan's map showed two piles of loose stones from the Seneca fireplaces after the fort had been destroyed. Stones are heavy, and it makes sense that over the course of two centuries, they wouldn't have gone very far—perhaps being lifted a couple of hundred feet across the creek and used to construct a useless (though decorative) wall. The progress of the fireplace stones suddenly feels like an equation for the passage of time.

It is a disparate collection of things at the corner of Castle Road and Pre-Emption Road in present-day Geneva. The past pokes up through the present and is still surprisingly visible. But the burial mound itself is underwhelming. Its gentle slope suggests a septic bed, rather than a mass grave. This is because the mound has been greatly altered from its original size of two hundred feet in diameter by ten feet in height. A hundred years after Sullivan's army drove out the Senecas, members of the tribe still returned in the early fall, every year, to visit their dead. The people who then owned the corner of Castle Road and Pre-Emption Road would give them dinner when they arrived for their rites, and again when they were departing.[30] In 1955, when the tribe became extinct and there were no more members left to travel to the spot, archaeologists excavated the site. When they had taken their "artifacts," the burial mound was considerably smaller.

I don't find any apple trees buried in the undergrowth along the creek bed, but I do discover one standing on a patch of grass out back of the minimart. It is a large tree with a bifurcated trunk, and by measuring its girth, I estimate that it's somewhere around sixty years old. So if it is a descendant of the original Seneca trees (and even though it's in the right spot, this is still a big if), it would be the fourth or fifth generation of the original orchard. But it has a resemblance to the tree in the photograph from 1904, right down to the bifurcated trunk, so there is a possibility that it has descended from one of the Seneca orchard trees.

Someone cared for the tree at one point, as it has a cable wrapped around its split trunk, put there with the purpose of keeping the tree together and preventing the trunks from separating. But it's clearly been a while since the cable was placed—parts of it are buried under the bark, and the apple tree has grown over it.

I'm not sure what is or isn't currently private property and how much I'm trespassing, so I dart about, furtively conducting my measurements and taking photographs. I feel alternately like a detective and a crazy person. Several cars on Pre-Emption Road slow down while I am measuring the girth of the bifurcated tree with the sewing tape measure I keep in the glovebox of my car. I found it years ago lying in the middle of a road, and it has proven to be unexpectedly useful in a variety of situations.

As evidence of the Seneca presence, the apple tree is not as definitive as the pile of rocks/stone wall. I want the tree to be descended from the original Seneca orchard, but I don't know for sure that it is. The thing to do is to come back here in the fall and taste the apples it produces. That will give me an important piece of the puzzle.

Driving back to Canada, I look at all the stray apple trees along the sides of the road, the blossom flashing white, and I think of how the trees operate as a kind of code or language into the past. A few trees clumped together signal an old orchard, while a single tree by the side of the road could be from an apple core flung from a moving vehicle; a lone tree in a cow field is perhaps the result of an apple being eaten and then excreted by a cow. The past is all around us if we look carefully and can figure out a way to read it.

Because tribes moved around, and because there were not the border distinctions that there are today, it can be assumed that within the Iroquois nation, agricultural practices would have been similar among those on the northern and southern shores of the Great Lakes.

In the east of what is now Canada, French Acadians introduced the apple to the Mi'kmaqs, who, having no name for it in their language, called it a French cranberry.[31] They planted "field-orchards" in Annapolis and King Counties, and became known for a variety of apple called the Mic-Mac Codlin.[32] This was an internationally recognized variety and was included in a report to the Royal Caledonian Horticultural Society in Edinburgh in 1885.[33]

The Indian orchards resulted in new and distinct varieties of apples. Over a dozen varieties that originated in indigenous orchards showed up as recognized apples in nursery catalogues and government horticultural reports. And it is here that I have to question the notion that the indigenous peoples only planted apple trees from seed and did not graft, as has been believed. To produce such distinct and flavourful fruit that was in wide circulation seems to suggest there was indeed some grafting going on. And why, if there was sufficient contact between the indigenous peoples and the settlers to introduce the various tribes to apples, wouldn't there have been some settlers who showed the indigenous peoples how to graft?

Among horticulturalists there was discussion about whether the indigenous practice of not pruning orchards was preferable to the methods used by the white settlers to keep their own orchards healthy and vibrant. "The old apple orchards planted by the Indians were found in good, sound condition," observed one report, "and continued so much longer than trees planted in later years by the white settlers."[34]

In an 1871 list of apples, rated in order of

desirability, the New York State Agricultural Society ranked the summer apple Indian Rareripe second after the Early Harvest. It was described as being "a fair apple and good bearer," and one of the best apples in terms of its suitability to the soil and climate of North America. It was further described in the report as being a "tart, pleasant apple [that] cooks well."[35]

In Georgia, there was an apple grown in the Cherokee orchards called the Equinetelle. It was in nursery catalogues until 1890, when it was renamed the Buckingham.[36] The Buff was also a Cherokee apple, as was the Nickajack, which was named after the creek where it was grown. Indian orchards were often beside rivers or creeks, and were frequently named after them. Both the Buff and the Nickajack are still being produced as heirloom apples in select orchards across North America, as is the Lawver, which originally was "found in an old Indian orchard in Kansas."[37]

The majority of the old indigenous apples are, however, extinct.

The Cullawhee came from Jackson County,

North Carolina, and was once the largest apple ever grown. A single apple measured twenty-one inches in circumference.

The Indiahoma was described in a Texas nursery catalogue from 1920 as having been discovered in old Indian Territory. It was a large, red oblong apple of excellent flavour.

The Indian Winter was listed in nursery catalogues in Georgia, Kentucky and Massachusetts from 1861 to 1878.

The Kittageskee, an extinct Cherokee winter apple that once grew in North Carolina and Georgia, was described as being of excellent quality, although it was judged too small to make a profit at market.

Other extinct Cherokee apples were the Red Warrior, the Spann and the Stevenson Pippin.

The Tillaque was a large, yellow-skinned winter apple from North Carolina. Its name meant "big fruit" in Cherokee.

The Coopers Russeting, first documented in Gloucester County, New Jersey, was thought to be of First Nations origin.

The Townsend was found in 1760 in a clearing in Bucks County, Pennsylvania. It was described as excellent for eating fresh, and also for cooking and drying.

The Tell was a red winter apple from Arkansas, and the Wall, another Cherokee variety, was also a winter apple. It was listed in an 1853 issue of *Western Horticulture Magazine*, where it was described as a prolific bearer.

In a letter to the editor of the journal *Southern Cultivator*, a man named Silas McDowell wrote the following: "Equineley, Junaluskee, Camack's Winter Sweet, Maverick's Winter Sweet, Cullasaga, Elarkee, Ducket, Nickajack, Cullawhee. The foregoing . . . apples were nearly all originally found growing in old Cherokee Indian fields, and I have thought it best to give each one the Cherokee name of either the Indian or the stream where it originally grew."[38]

Not many of the early settlers seemed to share Silas McDowell's sensitivity, and it appears that most apple varieties in the indigenous orchards were either renamed when the whites took over the land or left to go extinct.

One story with a somewhat happier ending involves the Junaluska—a yellow-skinned, medium-sized apple with russet patches and juicy yellow flesh. It was named for the chief of the Eastern Cherokees, who fought with Andrew Jackson against the Creeks and saved the future president's life, only to be driven out of his home in 1838 as a result of Jackson's Indian Removal Act. Chief Junaluska was initially imprisoned at Fort Montgomery, and then was forced to march with his people to eastern Oklahoma, a trek of some eight hundred miles. After several years there, he walked back by himself to North Carolina at the age of sixty-seven and petitioned the government to remain there. His service to Jackson was finally acknowledged, and he was given a piece of land near Robbinsville.

A tree bearing his eponymous apple was part of a Cherokee orchard there that the US government was intent on purchasing.[39] The chief didn't want to part with his favourite apple tree, and so the state commissioners gave him an extra fifty dollars for it. The land where the tree grew eventually became part of Silas McDowell's orchard, where he continued to grow the historic Cherokee varieties and sell them. He sold the Junaluska apple until 1859, but after his death the orchard was not preserved and the varieties there were left to grow wild.

In 2001, a North Carolina apple hunter, Tom Brown, found what he determined to be the Junaluska apple on land that was several miles from the historic Silas McDowell orchard. Through research and interviews, Brown was able to accurately identify the apple and he grafted three trees, which were subsequently planted at Chief Junaluska's grave near Robbinsville.

Here I must say that I found more examples of indigenous southern apples than northern ones because of the work done by apple hunters Tom Brown and Lee Calhoun; for over thirty years, Calhoun produced the definitive encyclopedia of old southern apples by painstakingly tracking varieties through nursery catalogues and oral histories. The same intensive research hasn't been conducted for northern apples, and it is also very hard to trace varieties when the names have been changed, as happened when the Equinetelle became the Buckingham. Also, if an apple wasn't sold commercially, it won't be in nursery catalogues. And many apples from indigenous orchards were never recorded by the incomers.

It is all down to names and naming. Anything I have been able to discover has been because there was a name to point me in a certain direction. It is no secret now that white settlers very effectively overlaid their culture on North American indigenous society and made the latter all but disappear. Where a name has survived to show us what once existed, I feel that name is still there because it was a way for the white settlers to remember a place, not because they were memorializing the indigenous use of that place. An "old Indian orchard," for instance, would become known to the settlers by that name, and to change the name would be confusing for them. A case in point was the "Indian Orchard" Girl Scout camp that existed in the early 1950s on the west shore of Cayuga Lake in New York State.[40]

I researched the location of old Indian orchards by looking at early maps and gazetteers for individual states and provinces in the United States and Canada, checking for place names that bore that description. I also looked at old horticultural reports, which often had very detailed accounts of where particular varieties of apples were growing. In this way, I was able to determine the sites of these old orchards.

There are currently two locations with the name Indian Orchard in the United States—one is a neighbourhood in Springfield, Massachusetts, and the other a village in Wayne County, Pennsylvania. There is also an Indian Orchard Campground in Webster, New Hampshire, and an Old Indian Orchard Cemetery in Indiana. There's a Cherokee Orchard Road in Gatlinburg, Tennessee, and a road called Sioux Orchard in Orange County, Tennessee. In New Jersey, there's a Cree Orchard Avenue. There's a Cree Orchard Point in Weems, Virginia, and a Cree Orchard Crossing in Tyron, Pennsylvania. In Rhineland, Wisconsin, there's a road called Chippewa Orchard, and in Texas there's a Muskogee Orchard Road. In both the Great Smoky Mountains of Tennessee and Fairview, North Carolina, there's a Cherokee Orchard Road.

These are the only names that have survived as markers for the old indigenous orchards. Like the varieties of apples themselves, many more names have likely been changed or left to go extinct.

This summer there was a long drought in Southern Ontario and upstate New York. The old tree behind the mini-mart in Geneva did not produce any apples, so I was unable to taste them, unable to determine whether they were descended from the Seneca orchard. This task will now, unfortunately, have to wait until next year.

Even though so much has disappeared and changed—the old orchards are gone, as is the memory of them—there are some positive developments to report. The present-day Oneidas in Green Bay, Wisconsin, have started what they call an "integrated food system," which includes an apple orchard, a farm, a store and a cannery. In their statement of purpose, the Oneidas outline their belief that the current mass production of food is damaging to the earth and to any sense of community, and they advocate for a return to small and local production. They assert, "Our food can be one vehicle through which we reassemble our fragmented identities, reestablish community and become native not only to a place but to each other. We find this vision of people living well and responsibly with each other and with the land on which they are placed to be deeply appealing."[41]

ANN
JESSOP

I was curious about the apple tree I'd found in back of the ruined cabin, and I wanted to discover more about the delicious White Winter Pearmain. How had an apple I'd never heard of ended up in my particular pocket of Southern Ontario? It seemed an impossible task to determine the apple's thirteenth-century beginnings in Norfolk, but surely, if the fruit had made the journey to America, I could find out who had brought it over from Europe.

My first research forays yielded the information that the White Winter Pearmain was one of several apple varieties taken as scions over the Mississippi

River in the saddlebags of a lone young man in the early 1800s. There was no mention of how the apple came to be in the southern United States in the first place, or why it was being taken west. After reading several similar accounts, I concluded that all the stories were versions of the same tale and had come from the same unacknowledged source.

It is the combination of the vague and the specific that often signals a lie. A man rode west of the Mississippi, his saddlebags filled with apple scions, in the early nineteenth century. No details of the man—where he came from, how he happened on grafts from English apple trees, why he was interested in propagating the trees. And yet, the very precise detail of the saddlebags filled with apple cuttings. The image is romantic and vigorous—a young man riding west to plant apple trees in the 1830s, during the time of the Indian Removal Act, when the indigenous peoples of America were being driven systematically from their lands to open up the west to white settlers, and their orchards were being burned to the ground or stolen from them.

But the story changed when I discovered from an apple encyclopedia[1] that it probably wasn't a man who went west to grow apple trees but a woman. An old woman. A Quaker. And this same woman had journeyed to England in the late 1700s and brought back apple scions from trees there, and had planted numerous orchards throughout the southern states. Because of this, she became known as Annie Appleseed—and predated Johnny Appleseed by almost fifty years.

Ann Jessop (sometimes known as Ann Jessup) was born Ann Matthews on October 10, 1738, to Walter and Mary Matthews in North Carolina. Ann grew up in a Quaker household, and in 1758 she married John Floyd. They had one child, Elizabeth, before John died after several years of marriage. Ann then became a Quaker minister in New Garden, North Carolina, in 1765. A year later she married Thomas Jessop, a man twenty-three years her senior who had eleven children from two previous marriages. Ann and Thomas had three living children together—Jonathan, Hannah and Ann—bringing the total number of youngsters for whom she was in some way responsible to an astonishing fourteen.

Thomas died in 1783, and the following year, Ann moved with her children to York, Pennsylvania (although she seems, from the minutes of the New Garden Quaker meeting house, to have returned later to New Garden). In 1817, she travelled on horseback, with her apple scions, to Ohio and lived with one of her children, Hannah, until her death in 1822 at the age of eighty-four. This was an incredibly long life when the average woman in the early nineteenth century died at fifty-six.[2]

It would seem that Ann's life could have easily been defined by her prodigious brood, or her passion for Quakerism, or her longevity. But it was an event in 1790, when she was fifty-two years old, that led to her greatest, and most lasting, achievement.

Quakers are pacifists, and when the Revolutionary War started in 1775, they refused to take sides. When the war came directly to New Garden, local Quakers tended equally to the American and the British wounded, turning their meeting house into a temporary hospital. The bloodstains apparently never came out of the floorboards, despite much scrubbing for months afterwards. And for years, a story circulated that there were bloody handprints on the walls of the meeting house from the suffering wounded. (The prints proved to be from the men who had built the structure and had used red chalk to measure the boards.)

The Battle of New Garden, on March 15, 1781, began at sunrise and lasted most of the morning. It was a precursor to the Battle of Guilford Courthouse—farther down the road—fought later that same day. These battles were part of the ongoing conflict between the British commander, Lord Cornwallis, and General Nathanael Greene, both of whom wanted control of North Carolina and were convinced they had the support of the people there.

The courthouse was ideal for a battle because it was at the centre of several roads, and these roads could be used for shuttling supplies, and for beating a retreat, if necessary. One of the roads went right through New Garden and past the Quaker meeting house, so it can be assumed that the battle there was a strike in advance of the later battle.

The men in charge of the cavalries that day—Lieutenant Colonel Henry Lee for the Americans and Lieutenant Colonel Banastre Tarleton for the British—were the favourites of their respective commanders, and both were in their mid-twenties, handsome, well educated and proud. They had fought each other before and had an ongoing hatred. There were three skirmishes—or "bouts," as they were called then—during the morning of March 15. At some point, Lee was thrown from his favourite horse, and that horse was captured by the British and subsequently ridden into battle by Tarleton, which must have been very galling to Lee and speaks volumes as to the men's competitiveness and familiarity with each other.

There is no accurate tally of the dead and wounded from the morning's battle, but British casualties were higher in number. A conservative estimate puts the combined death toll at between 125 and 150 men, with as many as 180 wounded for both sides.[3] The Quaker meeting house became a hospital when the armies pulled out, and was run by a British army surgeon and his two assistants. They were severely understaffed, so the more seriously wounded were cared for in the homes of New Garden residents. There must have been some mixed feelings about this, as the people of New Garden had suffered food raids from both sides for weeks before the battle, leaving some of the local farmers destitute.

The Quakers of New Garden tended the wounded for many weeks, neglecting their own farmwork in the process and also dealing with an outbreak of smallpox.[4] One of the unexpected consequences of having soldiers in their houses was that Thomas Jessop's daughter Sarah fell in love with a wounded British officer. Her father was furious at this turn of events and disowned her. This was a lasting state of affairs, and in his will two years later, Thomas left Sarah only five shillings—enough to buy two candlesticks, a small carpet or a cradle.[5] He left his other daughters, Hannah and Ann, "a feather bed, and furniture and at the age of eighteen or marriage, twenty-five pounds each."[6]

It was Ann senior who rallied around Sarah, accompanying her step-daughter and her new British husband back to England via sailing ship later in the year. Unfortunately, the officer succumbed to his injuries during the six-week voyage, but Sarah wasted no time becoming engaged to one of his friends, a member of the Scots Guards. When they reached port, she settled in Glasgow, Scotland, with James MacQueen, whom she married a few years later. Presumably, James and Sarah bonded over the death of Sarah's husband, and this helped their love along. Or because Sarah was already bound for Great Britain, they made the match for practical reasons.

Ann remained with the young couple while they established themselves, and then returned to visit them almost a decade later, well after Thomas had died. This time she spent two years travelling and preaching in the United Kingdom in the company of a British Quaker minister named Hannah Stephenson, who was also in her middle years. When Ann returned to North Carolina in 1792, she brought with her scions from a variety of apple trees, as well as a grain that was called English millet in Britain but became known as alfalfa when it was planted and cultivated in North Carolina. With the help of a young Quaker Friend, Abijah Pinson, who was good at grafting, Jessop set about establishing several orchards with the scions in the spring of 1793. Pinson eventually opened a large nursery in Westfield, North Carolina, where he sold seedling trees from the same British scions.

Because Ann Jessop travelled a great deal in her work as a minister, she was able to distribute apple trees among Quaker settlements in many of the northern and western states. In this way, and with the help of Pinson's nursery, she slowly populated America with her apple trees.

Who was Ann Jessop? There is virtually nothing with her direct stamp on it. She was a minister, and yet there are no sermons that survive (although one of her congregants described her as having a musical voice and a way of sermonizing that "was often a lofty style of blank verse, entertaining and interesting, holding an audience spellbound"[7]). If she had an interest in horticulture before travelling to England, that remains a mystery.

She had influence within her community, and influence within her family. Her son Jonathan was a renowned clockmaker and the postmaster for a period in Yorktown, Pennsylvania, as well as being a station-master on the Underground Railroad, but he kept on with his mother's work of propagating fruit trees and was responsible for developing the York Imperial apple. He had first called this apple Johnson's Fine Keeper, after the man on whose land he had discovered it, but he was persuaded by the famous landscape architect Andrew Jackson Downing (brother to the pomologist Charles Downing) to change the name. In a letter to Jessop, Downing says: "Friend Jessup.—I have received thy basket of very fine apples; it is the Imperial of late keepers, and very fine, and as thee says it originated near York, Pennsylvania, I would suggest the name of York Imperial."[8] (Fruit growing was in the Jessop blood in succeeding generations as well, with two of Jonathan's granddaughters going to California to start apricot orchards.)[9]

What becomes clear from looking through the monthly minutes of Ann Jessop's Quaker meeting house in New Garden is how much she liked to travel. She frequently applied for permission to "take the Truth" to other communities, both near and far. She seemed to be away more than she was home, and her trips, even to neighbouring communities, were lengthy. When she went to Deep River, for example, a mere ten miles away, she was often there for almost a month at a time.[10] She also travelled regularly to Virginia, New Jersey, Ohio, Pennsylvania, Maryland, Vermont and Indiana. A family biographer noted that Ann "was wont to make frequent journeys to the northern States in connection with her ministrations."[11] She clearly had the energy and the desire to venture outside of New Garden, and after Thomas's death in 1783, she also had the relative independence to do so. What is hard to separate out is how much of her travel was driven by religious fervour, and how much was simply wanderlust.

In 1797, Ann Jessop went to Virginia, Pennsylvania, Maryland and New York. In 1798, she went to Baltimore and journeyed along the eastern shore of Maryland, and the following year, she went back to Pennsylvania. Jonathan lived in Pennsylvania, so we can assume that she wanted to visit him as much as she did the Pennsylvania meeting houses. When Jonathan was just thirteen years old, she had taken him to Yorktown to apprentice him with a cousin as a clock- and watchmaker. They had travelled together in a covered Conestoga wagon,[12] "camping out at night, and keeping up a fire to drive off wild beasts."[13]

It is these little details that make Ann Jessop seem a bold woman, someone who sought out adventure and was not afraid of new experiences. The fact that her son remembered their journey to Pennsylvania and recounted it to his children and grandchildren means that it was memorable—not just a journey but an adventure.

The greatest adventure of all, however, was Ann Jessop's voyage to England in 1790, and her travels there with Hannah Stephenson. The Quakers required women preachers to work and travel in pairs. Because of this rule, female friendships were often of great importance, and single Quaker women frequently lived together as companions. Sometimes the bonds of female friendship were so close that the women involved manipulated their marriages around their friendships.[14]

There was a great deal of freedom in these arrangements that was not available in ordinary married life, and it is no surprise, really, that women preachers were often on the road. Still, Ann Jessop travelled more than most. And two trips across the Atlantic, with the second lasting a full two years, was quite a remarkable feat for an older woman in the 1700s.

When Ann arrived in England in the spring of 1790, the country was in turmoil over the French Revolution, which was stirring up heated debate on everything from lower taxes to assistance for the poor to larger questions of the inherent rights of humanity. In 1793, France would declare war on Britain, inciting a rebellion within the British Navy, a revolt in Ireland and riots to protest the depressed economic conditions brought on by war. So the country that Ann arrived in and journeyed through was in a state of agitation and flux, and she would not have been immune to, or ignorant of, the ideas that permeated this society at the time—especially as she was travelling with an Englishwoman. It can be assumed, because she remained in Britain for a full two years, that the political atmosphere either didn't bother her or excited her.

Hannah Stephenson was born into a Quaker family on July 15, 1745. For the first seven years of her life she lived in Whitehaven, and then her family moved to the Isle of Man, where they were the only Quakers. According to a small biographical sketch published by the Quaker society in 1845,[15] she was tormented by many temptations on the Isle of Man, yet fought through them and was rewarded with a visitation of "divine love."

Hannah's father died when she was seventeen, and the following year she went to Birmingham to live as a servant. She then moved to Essex and lived with a woman who owned a shop there. After that she resided with the family of Sarah Beck, who became a close friend and was a Quaker minister. Hannah became a minister herself at the age of twenty-two, and her services were described as "lively."

Though based in Essex, Hannah also liked to travel. In 1771 she went with Sarah Beck to London, Kent and Buckinghamshire. In 1778 she went to Surrey, Sussex and Kent, as well as Suffolk, Norfolk and Norwich. That same year she went back to London, and then later to Tottenham. From 1778 until she travelled with Ann Jessop in 1790, Hannah was constantly on the road, visiting most of the counties in England. Her travels with Ann are described as "a long northern journey, which extended as far as Glasgow,"[16] where presumably Ann visited with her step-daughter Sarah.

Hannah Stephenson never married. After Ann's return to North Carolina, she continued to travel throughout the British Isles, often in the company of Deborah Townsend, who was described as her "beloved" and "very intimate" friend. Stephenson died of a "lingering illness" in 1804, at the age of fifty-nine, and as was the rather bizarre Quaker custom of the time, her last words were carefully recorded. Because she lingered so long, she had many last words. Sometimes she complained about her discomfort; sometimes she extolled in the virtue of the Lord. Often she remarked on the sweetness of something she had just eaten. But finally she said, "Rejoice evermore, and in everything give thanks," and quietly slipped away.

Sadly, it is impossible to know the details of the long northern journey of Ann Jessop and Hannah Stephenson. But we do know that Ann Jessop came back to North Carolina two years later with seeds for English millet (alfalfa) and the scions of approximately twenty different apple varieties.[17] This means, at the very least, that she ate some apples on her English tour. She passed through or visited some orchards. She was made aware of the splendid properties of certain kinds of English fruit, and she desired to reproduce this fruit for her own people. And perhaps, in planting and eating the apples back in America, she was able to savour, once again, her time in England. Certain foods create, just by the act of tasting them, involuntary memories. Think of Marcel Proust launching his fleet of autobiographical tomes on the taste of a single madeleine.

Did Ann Jessop have an interest in apples before she went to England? Did she ever consider propagating fruit before? Or did her passion for apples come out of her experiences travelling through Britain and Scotland with Hannah Stephenson?

I imagine Ann and Hannah stopping for the evening with a Quaker household in Kent—the evening sun slanting in at the windows, and the air outside drowsy with bees—and being given a Yellow Summer Pippin to eat as part of their meal. The sweet crisp of the apple was likely unfamiliar and intoxicating to Ann. It would have been easy, when praising the taste of the fruit, to ask for a cutting to take with her. Or she might have risen early and gone out to the orchard the next morning with a pocketknife to do the task herself.

Or, she and Hannah are riding in their horse and trap through the countryside. It is September and they can smell the ripe fruit heavy on the trees when they pass the orchards. They stop the horse. One of them climbs down from the cart and plucks several apples to take with them on their journey. This time a Russet and a Limbertwig. The rough texture of the Russet's skin puts Ann off at first, but Hannah reassures her of the taste, and when Ann bites through the dry leather case, she is greeted with a rich, mellow juiciness beneath.

Or, in the heat of the summer of 1790,[18] Ann Jessop can't sleep and walks out of her host's abode into the garden that surrounds the house. She strolls under the apple trees, sampling the fruit from each one, and because she can't sleep and does not want to go back to the stifling house, she passes the time cutting scions from those trees where the fruit is most pleasing and fully ripe.

Among the apples that Ann Jessop took back to America were the Russet and the Limbertwig, as well as the Father Abraham, the Red Pippin, the Jannette (or Neverfail), the Striped Pippin, the Red Romanite, the Yellow Summer Pippin, the

Leathercoat, the White Winter Pippin, the Striped Horse, the Speckled Pearmain, the White Winter Pearmain, the Vandiver, the Pearwarden, the French Pippin, the Red Winter Pearmain and the Golden Russet.[19] They were a mix of cooking and eating apples and had a ripening range from July to January. Ann Jessop probably chose these apples because they could form the basis of an orchard. At least half were winter apples, and of those, most were good keepers and would last right through to spring. Apples could be picked fresh from the trees for that seven-month period and used for eating or cooking while they were at their tastiest. Some of the varieties, like the Russet, were fairly disease-resistant.

One of the apple scions that Ann Jessop brought back with her from England was the White Winter Pearmain—the apple that I had found growing on the old tree behind the deserted log cabin. In a nursery catalogue from North Carolina in 1870, the White Winter Pearmain was described by the state's leading pomologists as "the highest flavored apple in cultivation."[20]

The English apples that Ann and Abijah Pinson planted proved to be very popular and sold widely across the state, with many of the North Carolina Quakers grafting orchards for themselves. A nursery was started in Lynchburg, Virginia, to sell seedlings from the English apples, and another nursery was opened near Philadelphia for the same purpose. Through the early decades of the nineteenth century, grafts of the original apples were carried by Quakers and planted in Ohio, Indiana, Illinois and Missouri—and eventually every state and territory west of the Mississippi.[21] Most of the southern and Midwestern states were planted with apples that had originated with Ann Jessop's English scions.

Abijah Pinson, the man who helped Jessop set up her original orchard, was the son of Richard Pinson, a Quaker renowned for his eccentricities. He would not wear coloured cloth or use paper money. He didn't believe in owning land and refused to pay taxes. And he was very punctual in all his habits, both business and personal—so much so that when he was sick and feeble and unable to rouse himself from his bed, his horse, so used to the standard routine, would leap the pasture fence on meeting days, walk to the meeting house by himself and stand under his usual tree for exactly one hour before returning home again.

The relationship between Ann and Abijah was long-lasting. Not only did they work together, taking grafts and planting orchards, but Abijah married Jessop's daughter Ann.

When Ann Jessop returned from England, she was fifty-four years old, the age that I am now. It is a beguiling age, where the limits of life and energy are apparent, but also where there is still the drive and desire to start again, to have a second act. It's the late summer of life, Joanne liked to say. And just as flowers will sometimes bloom again in August or strawberries have a second harvest, human passions can run high in the fifties. Not for the last time, but perhaps for the last time when there is still the energy to cater to those desires.

Ann Jessop left on her travels to England as a Quaker minister, and she came back as a pomologist.

She worked with Abijah in planting orchards—the hard, physical work of digging and setting trees, and then maintaining them with pruning and burning the dead wood. She used apples as a form of commerce, to support herself and her family. In a sense it became the family business, with son-in-law Abijah running seedling nurseries and son Jonathan planting orchards in Pennsylvania. Even when Ann was seventy-nine years old and went to live with her daughter Hannah in Ohio, she took grafts of her English apple trees with her in her saddlebags and planted them west of the Mississippi.

There is nothing left of Ann in terms of anything she wrote, or said, or thought; what we have instead is something more intimate than any of that: her taste. She went to England and chose twenty apples, out of all the varieties that grew there in 1790, to bring back to America. She *chose* these apples—and that meant she tasted them, and she liked the taste of them above others. They weren't chosen simply for their practical advantages—the long-keeping winter apples, for example—as there were other apples with these same characteristics. This was the heyday of apples, and there were thousands upon thousands of varieties. No, Ann Jessop chose the apples that she liked the taste of, and that she wanted to continue to taste when she set up her own orchards back home in North Carolina.

It is an intimate act, tasting an apple—having the flesh of the fruit in our mouths, the juice on our tongues. Ann Jessop bites into an apple in an English orchard in the hot summer of 1790 in the middle of her life, and I bite into the same kind of apple in 2016, in the middle of my life, and taste what she did. For the time it takes to eat the apple, I am where she was, and I know what she knows, and there is no separation between us.

The log cabin and the dead apple tree led me to the White Winter Pearmain, which in turn led me to Ann Jessop. This is what happens with research. It opens up a world that you couldn't have imagined existed. And while it is impossible to trace the individual White Winter Pearmain trees that Jessop planted, it is perhaps not out of the realm of possibility to hope for some trace of her original orchards.

I drive down to North Carolina in late April. It is a journey from early spring to full-blown summer—a journey from the pink granite of the Canadian Shield to the dusky bloom of the Blue Ridge Mountains, ending in the lush greenery of North Carolina. I leave the scrawny woods of Southern Ontario, the trees still bare from winter, and arrive to the most majestic oaks I have ever seen, fully leafed out and hundreds of feet high.

This is a trip I might have made with Joanne. We travelled a lot together over the course of our twenty-year friendship. We went across Canada by train, to the Arctic and to New York City. We also had many short adventures closer to home, including a canoe trip down a long stretch of river in a pre-dawn world that included owls lifting over the water on their shadowy wings and deer sleeping along the edge of the riverbank. In fact, when I thought about Ann Jessop's trip through England with Hannah Stephenson, it reminded me of a journey, given a change of century and circumstances, that Joanne and I might have undertaken. I believe that Ann and Hannah must have had the same sort of easy companionship, to be able to travel so closely together for a full two years.

Joanne, being a poet, would have found much of her own material in a shared voyage to North Carolina.

When I get to New Garden, I find a new Quaker meeting house near the site of the old one, a low-slung brick building that replaced the original wooden meeting house where Ann Jessop was a minister. Nearby there is Jessup Grove Road, which leads to Jessup Lane, a short, tree-filled driveway that was probably the site of the original homestead belonging to Thomas and Ann.

In the cemetery out back of the new meeting house, I find the grave of Randall Jarrell, the poet, as well as the cornerstones of the original meeting house and several enormous oak trees. Near the centre of the cemetery is a bronze plaque commemorating the Revolutionary Oak, which used to grow there, and under which, in a mass grave, were buried the American and British dead from the 1781 battle. The tree was dynamited by vandals in 1955 to protest Eleanor Roosevelt's visit to the Guilford campus to talk about racially integrating public schools.

Tucked up against the trunks of other oak trees, some of which are two to three hundred years old, are grave markers from the early nineteenth century, including two marked "Jesup."[22] One grave is for M. Jesup, who died in August 1813, and the other is for D. Jesup, who died in May 1811. The stones are flat—stones that were likely found nearby—laid on top of the graves, but the real markers are, of course, the trees, which grow tall and strong, up out of the dead bodies, in essence becoming the new life-form for the dead lying entwined in their roots.

Standing under the oak trees, it is possible to imagine the time of Ann Jessop because the land on which the original meeting house stood remains in much the same condition as it was in the late 1700s. As a cemetery, it has been preserved from development. But the surrounding area has been overlaid by the roads and buildings of the twentieth century, making it impossible for me to catch a glimpse of the eighteenth beyond the names of Jessup Grove Road and Jessup Lane.

Jonathan Jessop was ten years old when the "skirmish" in New Garden took place between the British and American troops. He drew a detailed map of the event, showing the British camped near Deep River and the Americans near the Guilford Courthouse. He drew the battle near the courthouse in a starburst of red ink, perhaps to represent the blood. His house, where he lived with his father and mother, is also shown, and if his sketch is to be believed—which I am inclined towards because of the elaborate detail—the "skirmish" of New Garden happened directly outside their door. They would have had a full and intimate view of the fighting.

Ann Jessop's great-great-great-great-great-great-granddaughter, Emily, agreed to meet with me while I was in North Carolina, and generously spent a day driving around with me and looking for remnants of her ancestor's orchards. Because of the development

in the area, it seemed unlikely we would find anything there, but I had some hope for Westfield,[23]
where Abijah Pinson had his apple nursery, so we
drove an hour northwest, a journey of fifty-seven
miles—which in Ann Jessop's time, with her means
of transport, would have taken two days.

Some of the roads in the Westfield area had
intriguing names (3 Dog Farm Lane, Beaverdam
Creek, Animal Farm Trail, Fishpond Road), but
two in particular—Jessup Grove Church Road and
Apple Blossom Lane—seemed to gesture towards
the bit of the past that I was interested in.

We started with Jessup Grove Church Road.
I wondered if it had originally been called Jessup
Grove, with Church Road added on later, to indicate the presence of the twentieth-century Baptist
church that is there now. If the names had been put
together, it perhaps meant that the Jessup grove was
still in evidence at the time of the name change,
or that everyone in the area knew the road by that
name, so it couldn't easily be altered. (Interestingly,
in the same area is an Indian Grove Church Road,

which again seems to indicate that whatever the "Indian grove" was, it predated the newer Baptist church. The "grove" in that case could have been a settlement, a grove of trees or even an apple orchard.)

There is no Jessop grove there now—only a scattering of young apple trees along the road, in no particular pattern. But there is a tree nursery, and there are large sections of cleared fields with nothing growing on them, indications that something used to be there. It is no small feat to hack a clearing out of the thick North Carolina forests, so those fields would have been cleared for a purpose. And perhaps the presence of the large tree nursery spoke to the earlier nursery belonging to Abijah Pinson. Often, the same enterprises appear on the same spot, sometimes with the present-day businesses having knowledge of the past ones, but sometimes not. It is as though the land itself has memory of how it was used. Or the location is specifically suited to one type of pursuit, and multiple people, in different times, simply have the same idea of what to do in that place.

We drove next to Apple Blossom Lane, a road

that didn't have a single apple tree on it—a fact I found heartening, because again there were these large cleared fields. It seemed that the large empty fields in a short stretch of road called Apple Blossom Lane meant they must have once been full of apple trees.

There were several impressive, sprawling houses on the lane, and one of the empty fields was for sale. The road petered out into a cul-de-sac, and we parked there for a while. There was a beautiful view, over the unsold field, of the thick green forest, and beyond that of a mountain I forgot to ask Emily the name of. The field had golden and orange tall grasses near the road, and short green grass behind that. It was easily over four acres—a size I'm familiar with because it's the standard for many Ontario farm fields.

Emily and I talked a lot that day, and by the time we were parked in Apple Blossom Lane, it had become clear to me that we had, weirdly, a great deal in common. We were both writers, but really that was the least of it. Our commonality ranged further than our professions, extending to personality traits, and even to the fact that she had just finished a book I was currently reading.[24]

I didn't know what to make of our similarities. I had very low expectations for my trip to North Carolina. I was excited about driving around with Ann Jessop's great-granddaughter times six, but I had no assumptions of liking her beyond that fact, and no sense of what our conversation might be. I didn't think I would find any remaining apple trees, because apple trees don't live much past a hundred years. Any I did find, in the spot where the original orchards once stood, would have come from the seeds of the first trees, and even that seemed an unlikely prospect. It is hard for two hundred years to pass without land being developed and trees disappearing.

I had come to North Carolina mainly to make a connection with Emily, who had been very generous in sharing information about Ann Jessop, and also to see the landscape. It was wonderful to drive around the back roads of Westfield and marvel in the beauty and exquisite lushness of the countryside, and to see all the Jessop graves in the Quaker cemetery, even though they dated from the nineteenth and twentieth centuries.

Ann Jessop was, I think, a strong woman. She had adventures and made bold choices. Emily is a strong woman, and it is not hard to see in her the strength of that bloodline. But here I wonder about what writing is or can be. There is a prophetic or mysterious quality to it sometimes—when you are on the track of something, and even before that, when you are attracted to a subject. It is a kind of magic, and this is the only way I can think to understand why I had more in common with Emily than almost any other person, intimates included, and why that didn't feel at all accidental. It is an odd sensation, when on the trail of research, to also feel that the research has, in a feeling that cannot be fully articulated, been on the trail of you.

The day we spent together was a gift, and I was lucky enough to recognize that while it was happening, which is also a gift.

At one point, when we were parked on Apple Blossom Lane, where there were no apple blossoms, Emily remarked on how hard it is to know what anyone is thinking. "You don't know what I'm thinking," she said, "and I don't know what you're thinking," which made it seem as though she was thinking something really interesting, when I was only wondering what kind of bird had made the nest I could see in the scraggly tree in front of the car. I was also wondering what the orange grass at the edge of the field was called, and I was thinking how beautiful the trees beyond that field were. I was a bit drunk on the appearance of summer after the long and seemingly endless Canadian winter.

But I didn't tell Emily what I was thinking, and she didn't tell me what she was thinking. Instead, I pointed out the beauty of the trees, although it was her landscape and she didn't need me to point anything out to her.

We talked and drove around, the day unspooling in conversation and the deep greens of the countryside, the sounds of birdsong, and a breeze stirring the leaves on the trees. I was entirely present, and yet at the end of the day I recalled almost nothing, which is how I imagine life goes.

For a while you remember the taste of the apple, but then you just remember that it was sweet.

Ellen Isham Schutt, *Malus domestica*, Limbertwig, 1914.

#18708
"Father Abraham"
from
James Dickie,
Massies Mill, Nelson Co., Va.   B. Heiges
10/28/99   11/28/99

Bertha Heiges, *Malus domestica*, Father Abraham, 1899.

33253
Vandiver
Mrs. A. N. Berard,
Belair, Harford Co.,
Md.

12/30/04

B. Heiges

3/13/05

Bertha Heiges, *Malus domestica*, Vandiver, 1905.

33402
Golden Russet of Western (N.Y.)
W.H. Hart
Arlington
Dutchess Co. N.Y.

D. G. Passmore
2.3.05
2.27.05

Deborah Griscom Passmore, *Malus domestica*, Golden Russet, 1905.

USDA
WATERCOLOUR
ARTISTS

Because of the great number of apple varieties in America in the late nineteenth century, the United States Department of Agriculture (USDA) decided to create a Division of Pomology to collect and disseminate information about apples to fruit growers. The division opened on July 1, 1866, under the stewardship of the USDA's first agricultural commissioner, the rather ironically named Isaac Newton, who was a former dairy farmer from Pennsylvania known for his successful farming practices. Newton was appointed commissioner in 1862 by President Abraham Lincoln, who himself had a farming background, albeit a modest one. The Newtons and the Lincolns knew one another. The butter eaten at the White House was supplied every week by Isaac Newton's dairy farm, and he and his family had a close and ongoing relationship with the president.

Newton was sixty-six when he became agricultural commissioner, and his appointment was greeted with ridicule because his friendship with Lincoln was no secret in Washington. His age and lack of experience were questioned by many critics, as was his practice of hiring family members. (He hired one of his sons to run an experimental farm, and twice appointed a nephew to be chief clerk of the USDA.) In a report at the Fruit Growers' Convention in California, he was called a "great ponderous barnacle,"[1] and was laughed at when he issued his first report without binding it. (The loose-leaf pages were promptly used all over Washington grocery stores as wrapping paper for produce.)[2]

But Newton persisted with his plans for collecting and disseminating agricultural information.[3] He believed that "the best farmer is always the most intelligent man, and a community of knowledge is one of the strongest ties that can bind and bless society."[4]

When the Division of Pomology began, it was overwhelmed with requests from farmers to identify apple trees on their property, and so Newton decided to create an illustrative library to help with this task. He hired over fifty watercolour artists to produce accurate paintings of all American fruit. The artists began working in 1887, and when the effort was brought to a close in 1940, they had produced an astonishing 7,584 detailed paintings of different varieties of fruit and nuts, including 3,807 paintings of apples.

My grandfather did some botanical illustration for a time, painting examples of fruit and vegetables for seed catalogues in Britain. He was a lifelong artist, having studied painting at the Slade School of Fine Art in the 1920s and, because he had a family to support, moving into commercial art in the early heady days of advertising, before the camera replaced the artist.

Seed catalogues had regard for the artistic rendering, rather than the realistic reproduction. This is still true today. At least half the seed packets I bought last year for my garden had a hand-painted illustration on the front. This must be less a mere tradition than a tried-and-tested marketing strategy. There is something in the hand of the artist that makes a painting of a fruit or vegetable more appealing to a customer than a photograph. Perhaps it's because a photograph is so absolutely what it is—there are no subtleties. And to have a photograph of a carrot on a seed packet would be offering a promise that the carrots grown from those seeds would look exactly like the picture. A watercolour or a coloured pencil drawing of a carrot, on the other hand, tells you that this is an approximation of what the carrot you grow will look like. There are no promises made. This is what the artist thinks the carrot you grow might resemble.

The USDA illustrations of apples were done by twenty-one artists, nine of whom were women. Because I am tracing the history of the White Winter Pearmain, I will focus on the artists who painted examples of this particular variety. These artists considered each apple carefully before painting it, and perhaps there is something to be learned from their studies. Also, the USDA Pomological Watercolor Collection belongs to the golden age of the apple in North America, and it's worth looking at with that in mind. The renderings are beautiful, and while the artists are lost to history, as are many of the apples they painted, I want to honour their act of cataloguing the fruit and show a time in recent history when art and science worked side by side and were equals.

Bertha Heiges painted the first example of the White Winter Pearmain for the USDA, in 1898. Like all the watercolours, this one has two paintings of the apple on a single sheet of paper. In one painting the apple is shown whole, and in the second, directly below the first, it's displayed in cross-section so that the calyx, flesh and seeds may be seen.

Bertha Heiges's Pearmain is almost perfectly round in the illustration at the top of the page. It is yellow and freckled with brown spots on the left side, and covered with an orangey blush on the right. In the cross-section, the flesh is white and there are two seeds tucked together in the right-hand ovary near the core.[5] According to Heiges's handwritten note at the bottom of the picture, this particular apple was painted on March 2, 1898, and is from Coeur d'Alene in Idaho.

Bertha Heiges was born in Pennsylvania on June 29, 1866, to Samuel and Elizabeth Heiges. She was the second of their seven children. Her father was a botany professor, and in 1895 he became the chief pomologist for the USDA.[6] We can assume that this is how Bertha ended up painting apples for the Division of Pomology, as in 1895 she is also employed with the USDA as an "expert,"[7] making $600 a year. Two years later she is listed as a "clerk"[8] and is earning $1,000 a year—$200 less than another USDA watercolour artist, Deborah Passmore. That salary in 1897 is roughly equivalent to $29,000 today. (Passmore was the most highly regarded of the USDA artists, which accounts for the discrepancy.)

Bertha was college-educated and worked as an artist for the USDA until 1905, when she married Alexander Halstead Caldwell. They were married on October 18 in Virginia, where Bertha's father was now managing the Virginia State Test Farm for the USDA. According to the *Washington Post*, "The parlor [where the wedding took place] was beautifully decorated with autumn leaves, ferns, and shrubbery." Members of both families were present, indicating that the marriage was acceptable to all concerned. And Bertha's sister, Grace, played the piano—first Wagner's *Lohengrin* and later Mendelssohn's *Midsummer Night's Dream*.[9]

Bertha Heiges gave up her work with the Division of Pomology after her marriage. She and Alexander lived in Virginia before settling in San Diego for the duration of their lives. They were relatively old when they married—Bertha was thirty-nine, and Alexander forty-eight—so they did not have any children. Bertha didn't seek any other employment. She is listed on the federal census for 1910 and beyond as a "homemaker." Alexander worked as a clerk. He died on June 30, 1940, the day after his wife's birthday, at the age of eighty-three. Bertha lived on until 1956, when she died on May 26 at the age of eighty-nine.

These are the details of her life, the facts that are available through the public record. What is missing is her actual life. And so, I am left with a series of questions rather than any definitive answers.

Was she a committed artist? Did she delay marriage beyond her child-bearing years so she could give everything to her art? Did she continue to paint after she stopped working at the USDA? If so, where are her paintings?

Was her marriage happy? Was she expected to give up her employment and independence upon marrying? Did she want to?

What did Bertha and the other artists who worked for the USDA think about the ambitious project of creating a visual library of American fruit? Were they made to feel that it was important work? Did they feel this? Sometimes a painting of theirs was the only illustration in existence of a particular fruit.[10] Did this influence how they felt about what they were doing?

In the ten years Bertha Heiges worked as a watercolour artist for the USDA, she produced over six hundred paintings, each one signed in her spidery black hand in the bottom right corner of the image.[11] This is approximately one painting per week, an impressive output given that watercolours are made by layering colour upon colour, and that each layer has to dry before the next one can be applied.

I remember being at my grandparents' house when my grandfather was working on the seed catalogue. He painted upstairs in a small attic bedroom, at a drafting table under a window overlooking the back garden. He listened to the radio while he worked, BBC Radio 1, and he often recounted interesting things he had heard on various programs when he came down for supper at the end of the day.

When he was working on the seed catalogues, he would raid the fridge for specimens to draw or paint, much to the annoyance of my grandmother, who would watch the cabbage she had planned to use for supper disappear upstairs to become an artist's model.

My grandfather, like many of the USDA artists, also had a private artistic practice. He painted oils and watercolours, and made drawings, all through his life. He lived into his early nineties, and I have an oil painting he made at eighty-six that is as good as anything he ever did. When driving in the car, he would frequently lurch to a stop because he had seen an interesting tree or view, and he would sometimes make a quick sketch before returning to paint what he'd found. As an artist, he never stopped being interested in life, and that made him, always, a fascinating person to be around, because he lived in the present and was fully engaged with it.

Joanne was also an accomplished artist, in addition to being a writer. In the early days of our friendship, I asked her to teach me how to draw. We started with a plate of pears, because she said they were easy, given their pleasing shape. I don't think I was particularly good at rendering them, but I do remember her telling me to draw them as though I were touching their skin, and to try to work without lifting the pencil from the paper.

Years later, for a birthday, Joanne painted me a watercolour of a large yellow apple on a grey background—oddly enough, not unlike the White Winter Pearmain I ate outside the deserted cabin that day. Inside the card, she had glued fortunes from the cookies we used to get at the end of our weekly dinners at a local Cambodian restaurant.

You are next in line for promotion in your firm.

You will have no problems in your home.

Count to ten first. Then you'll know the urgency is real.

Amanda Almira Newton was born in 1860 and began painting fruit for the USDA in 1896, working for them until 1928, a full thirty-two years that took her from thirty-six to sixty-eight—an entire working lifetime. She was the granddaughter of Isaac Newton, the first agricultural commissioner of the USDA, although he died while she was still a child, so he cannot be charged with nepotism regarding her hire.

Amanda Newton painted over twelve hundred watercolours for the Division of Pomology, mostly of apples. She depicted the White Winter Pearmain multiple times, showing it in its unripe state, when fully ripe and just picked, and also after a few months of having been stored. Most of the exemplars were from California, although there was one painting of a ripe White Winter Pearmain from Idaho in which the apple is covered in spots and has patches of grey mould over parts of the skin.[12]

Clearly interested in how fruit changed and ripened with storage, Amanda Newton also created wax models of apples to show this evolution, and she exhibited these models at the Tennessee Centennial Exposition and at the World's Fair in St. Louis in

1904. Another USDA illustrator, Royal Charles Steadman, made and exhibited wax models as well, and it would seem that he and Amanda Newton had a friendship of sorts, as she commissioned him to paint a portrait of her grandfather.

Amanda Newton never married. She owned her own home in Washington, sometimes taking in a boarder, and listed herself as "head of household" and "artist" on the federal census of 1920.

She died in 1943, at the age of eighty-three.

In the one photo I could find of Ellen Isham Schutt, she is wearing a hat festooned with flowers across the brim. Her dark hair is piled up and she is frowning against the sun. She looks, if not exactly formidable, certainly very capable and confident. This is a woman who had a massive concrete house built on her father's land in Virginia and named it Ellenwood.[13] She was also the recording secretary for the Virginia chapter of the Daughters of the

American Revolution. She married twice and had no children. Her first marriage lasted only three years; her second was to a first cousin.

Schutt was born on April 15, 1873, in Oak Grove, Virginia. She worked for the USDA for ten years, between 1904 and 1914, and produced over seven hundred watercolours for them. Like Royal Charles Steadman and Amanda Newton, she made models out of wax to show the effects of storage on various types of fruit.

In 1911, Schutt was commissioned by the University of California to make a series of paintings that demonstrated how disease and long-term storage altered and marked apples. Over four years, she painted 286 of these watercolours of damaged fruit.[14] (Schutt painted the White Winter Pearmain in 1906, well before she began her series of commissioned watercolours. The Pearmain that she illustrated was all yellow and covered with small dots; the apple was from a tree in Colorado.)

Like many of the other artists who worked for the USDA, Schutt was in her thirties when she did most of her paintings—arguably the prime of life, when her technical skills, not to mention her eyesight, might have been at their sharpest. She died in Falls Church, Virginia, in 1955, at the age of eighty-two. She was remembered for her "artistic skill, patriotism, and civic dedication."[15]

When my grandfather was young and fresh out of art school, he spent a summer travelling around Britain, offering to repaint pub signs in exchange for food and lodging. In this way, he managed to spend months moving around the country on no money. Some of his repainted signs still hang outside of various country pubs to this day.

To be an artist is to be inventive—it's one of the requirements of the job—and in many artists, this innovation extends to their own lives as well. My grandfather had many schemes for earning money from his art: pub signs, cutout model villages, beer coasters, cigarette cards, brochures. He always had a plan afoot, an enthusiasm to chase down. I realize now, as I get older, that this is not unlike my attachment to my projects, and my need to throw myself whole-heartedly into the future and my latest story idea.

My grandfather belonged to an elite group of artists in the advertising world. It was a time where the advertising poster was held in high regard, with the more famous illustrators signing theirs, acknowl-edging the human component of the advertisement, and blurring the lines between commerce and art. One of the most renowned poster artists of all time was the French painter Henri de Toulouse-Lautrec.

There were many poster artists in Britain in the 1930s, and my grandfather remembered rushing out into the streets to see the new work of artists he admired, as excited as if he were viewing paint-ings in a gallery. He himself painted posters for London Transport, travel ads for Southern Railway and recruiting posters for the army. At the London Transport Museum, you can buy a reproduction of one of his posters informing you to have correct change for the bus conductor. All of his original posters are now sought-after items, sold through auction houses and beyond the means of anyone in his family.[16] He would have found that amusing, or appalling. I can't decide which. Like a lot of artists, he struggled financially all his life, never fully recovering from the arrival of the camera into the commercial art world. He worked for himself after that, doing smaller, less public work for smaller, less public clients—those who still valued a hand-drawn or painted illustration over the glossy perfection of the photograph.

Deborah Griscom Passmore was the most highly regarded artist for the Division of Pomology; she worked for the USDA for nineteen years and painted over fifteen hundred watercolours in that time. Her tenure ended only because she died of a heart attack in 1911, at the age of seventy.

Passmore was an artist whose reach extended beyond her paid botanical illustrative work. She had a private art studio in Washington and taught painting from there, and she produced hundreds of her own pieces outside of her employment. A friend remembers her as "a most inveterate sketcher [who] did literally hundreds of little bits of landscape in oil; when riding or walking she was everlastingly composing pictures."[17]

Deborah Passmore was born on July 17, 1840, the fifth and final child of a father who was a farmer and a mother who worked as a teacher and a Quaker minister. Deborah's mother died when she was small, and Deborah was raised by her eldest sister, Mary, and sent for her education to the boarding school where her mother had taught before she married. A spirited child, Deborah was interested in art right from the beginning; she even attempted to draw flowers using their own juices, which she got from chewing the flower and spitting out the liquid contained within to use as pigment.[18]

She studied art at the School of Design for Women and the Academy of Fine Arts, both in Philadelphia, and then spent a year in Europe looking at the great painters in the galleries there. Influenced by the English biologist and botanical illustrator Marianne North,[19] Passmore painted a folio of the wildflowers of North America[20] and was hired by the USDA in 1892.

Passmore lived an independent life, never marrying, and remained deeply immersed in the Quaker faith of her parents. She eventually owned her own home, where she lived with a succession of yellow cats and her vast collection of shells and coral.[21]

Deborah Passmore painted the White Winter Pearmain twice, once in 1908 and once the following year. The 1908 apple was very red, with almost no yellow on it at all, and was from California. The 1909 apple, from Idaho, was yellow with a deep red blush on the left-hand side. Both were beautifully luminous—Passmore was such a detailed painter that she often used a hundred watercolour washes on a single painting.[22]

Of the paintings she made of subjects other than fruit, she seemed to favour landscapes, with enticing paths leading the viewer through mature summer forests, or a depiction of a tranquil lake in a bowl of hills at sunset. She painted pleasing views from her jaunts or objects that were readily at hand, such as a paring knife, two reddish pears on a blue dish and an unopened tin can. It's interesting to note that she painted fruit in her off hours, not only when she was on the job.

When an artist begins painting in childhood and maintains a singular focus for her lifetime, there is a large part of her—the part doing the creating—that is private, unseen. And so it is a bonus to find this description of Deborah Passmore at work on a painting, written by a friend, and showing the intersection of the inner and outer worlds of this gifted working artist:

While painting she was quite oblivious to surroundings. She would sit in a greenhouse on an overturned box, her feet in the wet, and paint and neither see nor hear what transpired around her. Well I remember when she was painting the orchids of the White House for the Columbian Exposition; it was in August, 1892, and I went over to the conservatories to see how the picture was coming on; I found her working away in an orchid house, steaming hot as a Turkish bath. "Aren't you smothered, suffocated?" I asked. She never heard a word I said, but wiping her dripping face and pointing to the half-done picture with a look of affectionate adoration, such as only a mother is supposed to give her baby, she exclaimed: "Beautiful things, are they not?"[23]

After years of being an artist, or a writer, it is hard to separate who you are from what you do. I don't remember a day—a moment, even—when my grandfather wasn't painting or drawing or talking about art. I recall one conversation where he talked about Danish inventions, about how the Danes had invented many of the important items in our modern world—matches, lighthouses, yeast, the loudspeaker.

He would often hold up something at the grocery store—a package of biscuits or a pound of butter—and say, "An artist designed that label." Driving under a bridge, he would say, "An engineer built that, but an artist thought of how it should look." He believed, and made me believe, that the role of the artist was the most important in the world, and that the hand of the artist was everywhere and in everything. "Someone had to think of that," he would often say, about anything—a book cover, the design on a packet of tea. He was always appreciative of the creative efforts of other people, and always fired up about his own.

James Marion Shull was born on January 23, 1872, the elder of Harrison and Catherine Shull's two sons. James Shull worked as an illustrator for the US Forest Service from 1907 to 1909 before moving to the USDA; he worked there until his retirement in 1942, first as a botanical illustrator, and later as a botanist. He eventually became a fruit disease investigator, and many of his illustrations show diseased fruit rather than healthy specimens. Like Deborah Passmore, James Shull was also a Quaker. He had wide-ranging artistic passions, turning his hand to both writing and gardening, in addition to painting over 750 watercolours for the USDA.

Shull was also an iris grower and breeder, and later a judge for the American Iris Society. He wrote a book about the iris, for which he provided full-colour illustrations. In the preface, he said that on his half acre of land in Maryland, the iris had become "the dominant note in this suburban garden where a professional man sought solace and relaxation and healthful exercise in hours of leisure from his desk."[24] He was proud that he had sold his irises throughout America and as far afield as England.

After the First World War ended, Shull also wrote a rather poetic brochure with the idea of melting down the cannons used in the war and fashioning bells out of the metal. These bells would then form "peace carillons" for Washington, and indeed for every major city in Europe that had been affected by the war.[25] It would be poetic justice, he reasoned, as a great many bells had been melted down to make the cannons at the start of the war.

The White Winter Pearmain that James Shull painted for the USDA is a diseased and underripe apple, still green and yet covered with brown lesions on the outside, and having pockets of rotted flesh on the inside. This particular apple was from Washington State, and he painted it in 1913.

A few years after retiring from the USDA, James Shull died at home in Maryland, on September 1, 1948, at the age of seventy-six. He was a lifelong bachelor.

My grandfather fought in the Second World War. He was in a tank corps in North Africa and then in Italy. Like many of his generation, he spoke little about his war experiences, except to say that it was very hot and claustrophobic inside the tank. He had regular nightmares postwar, yelling and thrashing in his sleep, and once he told me that he hated the scent of lilacs because they reminded him of dead bodies.

He wasn't an enthusiastic participant in the army, often disagreeing with his superiors. He liked to say that there were two wars: "The English against the Germans, and Ronald Brett against the British Army." What kept him sane was the art he managed to do while he was a soldier. He carried a tin cigarette box of pastels in his breast pocket and made drawings of the camps where he was stationed. He was the war artist for his battalion, and some of his paintings and drawings from that time now hang in the Imperial War Museum in London, England.

Royal Charles Steadman, the last of the White Winter Pearmain artists, was born on July 23, 1875, in Portland, Maine. He was the second son of Alban and Emma Steadman, and his parents separated when he was still a boy.

Steadman studied art at the Boston Museum of Fine Arts and the Cowles Art School, and then attended the Rhode Island School of Design, taking a job after graduation as a jewellery designer for a commercial company. He also worked designing stage scenery and as an instructor at RISD. He even submitted several designs for postage stamps to the postmaster general.

In 1915, Royal Charles Steadman joined the USDA in the Division of Pomology, working as a botanical illustrator, and then later as a botanical artist. Like some of his contemporaries there, he had an interest in the effects of storage and cold on fruit, and he made many wax models to show the impact of these conditions. Steadman worked at the USDA until he retired in 1941, and during that time, he produced over nine hundred watercolours, as well as pen-and-ink sketches and wax models of fruit. He married three times, divorcing twice, and had one son by his second wife. He died on August 6, 1964, at the age of eighty-nine.

The example of the White Winter Pearmain painted by Royal Charles Steadman in 1918 is the most recent depiction of the apple in the USDA Pomological Watercolor Collection. The painting is done in a simple grey wash, with no colour in the apple and just one illustration of the fruit rather than the customary two. Steadman's apple is in cross-section and sits crookedly on the page, with a single seed in its left-hand ovary.

I think of my grandfather hunched over his desk upstairs in the rented house near Tunbridge Wells, painting a pea pod or a cabbage or a stalk of Brussels sprouts, arguing back at Margaret Thatcher on the radio. And I think of the USDA artists who went to work every day and painted apples. Making a painting from something real to be used to identify something real. The painting a little island where painter and subject existed together for the length of time it took to make the rendering. What did the USDA painters make of their subjects? What did they learn about apples from years of close observation? Were they happy to have a regular source of income, or did they regret not taking more of a chance on their art, not trying to make a career out of painting only what they wanted to paint?

When I was in my twenties and driving around with my grandfather on his errands, he confessed to me that he thought he'd made a mistake in not choosing to be a full-time painter. "But what could I do?" I remember him saying. "I had a family. It felt selfish. Like Gauguin going off to the South Seas."

At the Slade School of Fine Art, my grandfather had won a prize. He'd had his early work exhibited, and my mother still has a photograph of him, when he was a young man in his twenties, impossibly handsome, striding down a London street with his prize-winning painting tucked under his arm.

When my grandfather told me that he regretted his choices, I was living in England, giving myself the self-imposed test of remaining there for a year and trying to complete a novel, attempting to write every day to see if I could do it, if I was suited to the solitary life. That conversation galvanized me into becoming a full-time writer, into making writing the number-one priority of my life, into forming my life around my commitment to writing and into not having the same regrets as my grandfather. But of course, every choice has its sacrifices, and though my grandfather lived until I was forty, he didn't live long enough for me to be able to tell him that the life of a full-time artist is also full of regrets. They're just different ones.

None of the USDA watercolour artists in the Division of Pomology wrote about their experiences of painting apples for a living. Or if they did, those reminiscences didn't survive into this century. So I can only guess what that experience was like for them. But it's an educated guess, because my grandfather was engaged in a similar pursuit and I had the good fortune to observe him while he was making his illustrations for the seed catalogue.

What I remember was the liveliness around him—the voices from the radio, the birds outside his studio window. I remember his work surface cluttered with the tobacco tins he used to store pencils, and his many paintbrushes standing stiff and tall in an old can. I remember him rushing downstairs and rummaging through the fridge in a terrible hurry, then rushing back upstairs again with whatever fruit or vegetable he needed to paint. (Halfway down the staircase he'd attached a metal bar to the ceiling so he could hang by his arms for a few seconds whenever he descended the stairs, stretching out his back from all the hours hunched over his work table.)

I never saw him doing the illustrations. No one was privy to those moments. That was between him and his art—how he applied colour and light to the blank page, and made something that had once been alive come alive again. This was private and shared with no one. It was his business, his struggle, his pleasure, his meaning, his life.

R. C. Steadman.
8-28-'19.

Sweet Bough.
Expt. Station,
So. Haven, Mich.

Royal Charles Steadman, *Malus domestica*, Sweet Bough, 1919.

Bertha Heiges, *Malus domestica*, Red Astrachan, 1903.

59089
"Porter"
F. C. Sears
Amherst
Hampshire, Mass.

A. A. Newton.
9-30-12
10-1-12

Amanda Almira Newton, *Malus domestica*, Porter, 1912.

Deborah Griscom Passmore, *Malus domestica*, Quince, 1894.

#7420
Rec'd 9/12 '94
from E. P. Purington
West Farmington

Cole Quince

D.G. Passmore
Cole

ROBERT
FROST

The poet Robert Frost had a long relationship with apples. On the Derry, New Hampshire, farm that he owned for nine years, he worked an orchard that was the inspiration for his several famous poems about apples, including the much-vaunted "After Apple-Picking," which begins:

> My long two-pointed ladder's sticking
>   through a tree
> Toward heaven still,
> And there's a barrel that I didn't fill
> Beside it, and there may be two or three

Apples I didn't pick upon some bough.
But I am done with apple-picking now.

Although the farm in Derry was the source of much of Frost's poetry, he wasn't a very successful farmer, and in 1909, at the age of thirty-five, he sold the place. In 1912, after working briefly as a teacher, he moved his young family to England, intending to concentrate solely on his writing. It was a bold choice, but it paid off. He befriended Ezra Pound and Wilfred Wilson Gibson, moved his family north to Gloucestershire on their recommendation and had his book *North of Boston* reviewed three times in three different publications by the English poet Edward Thomas. Each of these reviews was equally laudatory, and together they were responsible for establishing Frost's critical reputation in England.

Frost and Thomas developed an intense friendship, and Thomas moved his own family to Gloucestershire to be near his new friend. He had been depressed before meeting Frost, working con-stantly at writing non-fiction books, reviews and articles to try to support his wife and three young children.[1] It was Frost who, after reading *In Pursuit of Spring*, Thomas's eloquent account of travelling through England by bicycle, convinced him that he really should be writing poetry.

Theirs was a friendship of cross-pollination. Thomas became a poet because of Frost—a poet of such renown that, years later, Ted Hughes would state, "He is the father of us all."[2] And Frost secured his own reputation as a poet because of Thomas's ecstatic reviews of his work, where he called Frost's poems "revolutionary."[3]

Their friendship had its zenith in 1914, particularly that summer. Frost said in a letter to his fellow poet Amy Lowell in 1917: "We were together to the exclusion of every other person and interest all through 1914—1914 was our year. I never had, I never shall have[,] another such year of friendship."[4] It was a sentiment shared by Thomas, who wrote in a letter to Frost on October 4, 1915: "The next best thing to having you here is having the space (not a void) that nobody else can fill."[5]

Thomas and Frost spent their time traipsing round the countryside in Gloucestershire, doing what Frost called "talks-walking." They shared a common idea of what poetry should be—that it should have musicality, but the musicality should come from both the sound of a sentence and the sound of the words placed within it, so that the two layers of cadence worked together, with the sound of the sentence imitating, on a subconscious level, the rhythm patterns found in everyday speech.

The summer of 1914 in England was magnificent, with many warm, sunny days, and the walks taken by Robert Frost and Edward Thomas were plentiful. In an article called "This England," published in the *Nation* on November 7 of that year, Thomas described finding "chiefly cider apples, innumerable, rosy and uneatable, though once or twice we did pick up a wasp's remnant, with slightly greasy skin of palest yellow, that tasted delicious."[6]

Apples were of interest to both men, and that yellow apple with its greasy skin reappeared in a poem that Thomas wrote of their friendship, "The Sun Used to Shine":

> We turned from men or poetry
>
> To rumours of the war remote
> Only till both stood disinclined
> For aught but the yellow flavorous coat
> Of an apple wasps had undermined.[7]

And later in that same poem, he sums up the friendship by saying:

>   like those walks
> Now—like us two that took them, and
> The fallen apples, all the talks
> And silence.[8]

Frost also immortalized the walks with Thomas in a poem called "Iris by Night," where he talks about the time they saw a circular rainbow, a miraculous occurrence in the short life of a miraculous friendship.

In the fall of 1914, Frost and Thomas sat on an orchard stile in Gloucestershire, on the day war began, and wondered if the guttural booms of the guns from across the Channel in France would soon be audible where they were.[9] In 1915, Frost returned with his family to America, with plans for the Thomas clan to join them there after the war, and for the men to take up farming together in Vermont. But Thomas increasingly felt that he should fight for England, and he joined up that same year. On April 9, 1917, at the age of thirty-seven, he was killed on the first day of the Battle of Arras. His battalion had been stationed in an orchard, and in a last letter to the poet Walter de la Mare, Thomas framed his chances of getting out of the war alive in terms of that orchard, saying, "We might see the apple blossom, but I doubt that."[10]

Years later, after the Second World War, Frost wrote about missing his friend in the essay "A Romantic Chasm": "I wish Edward Thomas (that poet) were here to ponder gulfs with me as in the days when he and I tired the sun with talking on the footpaths and stiles of Leddington and Ryton."[11]

I find it interesting that he has cribbed a line from the ancient lament of the poet Callimachus for his fellow poet and friend Heraclitus:

> They told me, Heraclitus, they told me you
>   were dead,
> They brought me bitter news to hear and
>   bitter tears to shed.
> I wept as I remember'd how often you and I
> Had tired the sun with talking and sent him
>   down the sky.[12]

One grief stands in for another. The friendship of one pair of poets has echoes in that of another pair.

Walking has always been a ruminating activity favoured by writers. Maybe it is the natural rhythm of walking—which happens in four-four time—that calls up a sympathetic cadence of words and ideas. Or maybe it is the act of movement after sitting at a desk all morning that helps to shake loose new thoughts and ways to express them. A writer walking alone has time for reflection, but writers walking together fall into discussion.

I used to walk with Joanne before she was ill. There was a time when we walked every day, and there was a season when our walking inspired and gave shape to our writing. Unlike Frost and Thomas, we walked mostly in winter, and the particular winter that influenced us was over a decade ago now.

The St. Lawrence River begins in Kingston and often freezes over. That winter it froze early and without much snow cover on it, making it perfect for walking on, and every day Joanne and I would trudge along the frozen river. Our walks took us along a mile or two of shoreline, both east and west, depending on our whims or mood, or the direction of the cold winter wind. We were on the ice at first freeze in December and off it at final thaw in mid-March, so we witnessed the progress of the season on its thick, then thinning, skin. We listened to the muffled boom of the trapped water shifting under the surface, and we saw the beautiful plates of blue-tinged ice piled up on one another near the shore. Walking east there were spots where streams had frozen on the faces of the scalloped banks, and the effect of the stilled movement was hypnotic and gorgeous. When the sun hit the frozen streams, they glittered and glimmered as though they were still moving.

Walking on the ice made the world new again. The shoreline was unfamiliar when seen from the perspective of the river, so we took to naming parts of it. Elephant Rock was a large glacial erratic that was tucked up against a small cliff where an enormous willow tree grew. From above, from the land, the boulder was invisible, but from the river it was gigantic, its pink granite surface in folds like the skin of an elephant. Old Man's Beard was one of the frozen streams that had adhered to the side of a small cliff. Dog Beach was the place where I took my dog to swim in the summer and was often our entry point onto the river—we could walk out gradually onto the ice there because there was no elevation change; it simply fanned out from the shore into the river.

That winter there was a wolf pack living in close proximity to Kingston.[13] In certain parts of the city, you could hear the wolves howling at night. One day when we were walking west along the frozen river, we found the mostly intact carcass of an adult deer a few hundred feet out from the shore. When we came back the next day, some of it had been eaten. We returned every day for a few days to gauge the progression of the feeding, but the wolves must have either been watching us or smelled us, because they soon left a sentry, a lone blackish wolf that watched us walk towards the kill and then away again, as we deciphered and heeded the message he was there to deliver.

Our triumph that winter was to walk over the ice from Kingston to Gananoque, a distance that was eighteen miles by road and, with all the bays and obstacles along the shoreline, considerably more along the river surface.

We did the walk in early March, when the days were lengthening into spring and the temperatures were warming up. The returning strength of the sun had made the surface of the ice granular, which made the walking easy because our boots didn't slip and slow us down. We were able to stride along the frozen river as quickly as we could a city street. But the warming temperatures had also made the ice unstable in parts, and we had to deke around melted sections, and sometimes even actual holes. We tried to keep close to shore so that if we did fall through, the water wouldn't be deep, but there were a few times when this wasn't possible and we were forced to walk across an open bay, our footsteps filling with water the moment our boots lifted up for the next step. Periodically people waved at us from shore and we cheerfully waved back, only to find out later that they were warning us off the soft ice, and that we made the news as a cautionary item about the ice being unsafe to venture out on.

We had a kicksled with us, to carry our supplies—lunch, extra socks and a flask of tea—and we started in the early morning so that we would have the whole day for the venture. I remember that there was a mist that morning, and that the trees and shrubs were coated in a thin layer of ice and sparkled in the sun as we set off from Dog Beach.

The sun shone all day. When we sat down, on logs or rocks, to eat or have some tea, it was as warm as May because the sun reflected off the ice. We walked without gloves or hats and with our coats open, and we followed the tracks of a lone wolf or coyote as it skirted the shore. When the tracks led across a bay rather than hugging the land, we followed, trusting in the judgment of the animal. The wolf or coyote didn't go as far as Gananoque, but almost, and it made me realize, and appreciate, the distance that predatory animals often have to travel to fill their bellies.

The walk took all day. We reached our destination by dinnertime, after over eight hours on the ice, tired but exhilarated, and then had a friend pick us up to drive us home. It had been a perfect day, and the things we had seen and learned from our winter of walking on the frozen river, and from this epic journey, made their way into stories and poems and paintings, fuelling our respective creative projects for years to come.

Shortly after that walk, Joanne wrote a poem about it and gave it to me:

I set down this account
of walking on the water
of the great river, week upon week
against a blue blaze,
laying down my text of footfalls
among notations of wolf and deer.[14]

Sometimes there are days, moments, that seem to fall out of the tight mesh of time and obligation, where we can live outside of our lives, slip the leash. That walk was one of those days, and because the weather and ice conditions have never been that ideal again, no one else has yet managed to duplicate our feat.

Weeks before she died, Joanne brought up our river walk. She wanted to know if I would ever try it again with someone else. I said that I wouldn't, that I would just let our record stand. The walk over the ice had remained, for both of us, one of the exploits of which we were most proud.

"I think that's a good idea," she said.

I feel, from the way Frost and Thomas wrote

about their walks in the summer of 1914, that they experienced a similar burst of glorious friendship, and that the symbols they took from those walks— the flavorous yellow apple, for one—were used as memorials to instantly bring back that time and place.

Robert Frost settled back into his farming life after England, for a short time in Franconia, New Hampshire, and then in Shaftsbury, Vermont. When his wife, Elinor, died in 1938, he started dividing his year, with winters spent first in Boston and later in Cambridge, Massachusetts, and summers spent at a newly purchased farm in Ripton, Vermont. He had orchards in both Shaftsbury and Ripton. The apple orchard at the stone farmhouse in Shaftsbury was meant to be the sustaining crop of the farm. The trees planted by Frost and his son Carol there included McIntosh, Northern Spy, Golden Delicious, Red Delicious and Red Astrachan.[15]

Frost was becoming more famous by the 1920s, and he didn't return to farming with his previous vigour, leaving the orchard in Shaftsbury mostly in the care of Carol. The apples cultivated by Frost and his son were popular commercial varieties for the time and place. It was a fairly standard orchard, while the one outside his writing cabin in Ripton, Vermont, is more personal. The cabin is on the property of the farm that Frost used as a summer home for the final twenty-four years of his life.

Frost had not returned to England since he left in 1915, but in May 1957, at the age of eighty-three, he went back to receive honorary degrees from both Oxford and Cambridge. While he was there, he returned to his old haunts in Gloucestershire, accompanied by his granddaughter Lesley and a photographer from *Time* magazine. He even went to the house where Edward Thomas had stayed, but he didn't want to go inside. "Instead he walked to the nearby orchard where the men had spent many hours together, and after 10 minutes, walked silently back to his car."[16] There's a photo taken of him standing in a field where he used to walk with Thomas, one hand covering his face to hide his emotion from the photographer.

At that point in his life, Robert Frost had lost almost everyone—Thomas, Elinor and four of his six children had all died before him. In one of his notebooks, he wrote, "I left myself in England and went back looking for myself."[17] And in another notebook, one he kept when he was first in England, he observed, "Curl most significant thing in nature. Things return upon themselves."[18]

When Frost returned to America, he set about planting his last orchard near his writing cabin in Ripton. He began having discussions about the orchard with a local nursery the previous December, but the apple varieties weren't finalized and grafted onto the wild trees until June 1957.

The nursery in Shelburne, Vermont, worked with the renowned heritage apple enthusiast Ira Glackens (also a painter and writer, and the son of the realist painter William Glackens) to get Frost the apples he wanted. His desired varieties included

Red Astrachan, Porter, Sweet Bough, Sops of Wine, Montreal Peach, Red Van Buren, Cole's Quince, Gravenstein, Jefferis and St. Edmund's Russet.[19] He had wanted two trees each of all those varieties, except for the Gravenstein and Jefferis, of which he wanted only one. But the varieties available at the time from Glackens were fewer in number, and the trees that Frost eventually selected for his orchard included just six varieties—Sweet Bough, Red Astrachan, Cole's Quince, Jefferis, Lowland Raspberry and Porter.[20] There was no White Winter Pearmain in the mix, but it had become a less popular apple by Frost's time. Refrigeration had undermined the usefulness of winter apples, much as the camera made the watercolour artist redundant.

The Sweet Bough is an early nineteenth-century apple of American origin. It is medium to large in size and has pale yellow skin and white flesh. Not a good keeper, it is best eaten fresh and has a crisp honey flavour. It has been called the best-tasting early sweet apple. It ripens at the end of July or early August.

The Red Astrachan is another apple ripening in August. It is of Russian origin and was introduced into North America in the early nineteenth century. It was a very popular New England apple in Frost's time, although it is now hard to find. Also not a good keeper, it is best cooked and is said to make the best jelly of all the apples. It is a medium apple and yellow in colour, with streaks sometimes so numerous that it can appear to be solid red.

Cole's Quince is a yellow ribbed apple with grainy flesh that, when fully ripe in August, has the taste of quince to it. This large apple is used primarily for cooking and does not store well. It is an old Maine variety and was discovered there in 1806.

Jefferis was a variety once popular with home orchardists because it ripened progressively, a few apples at a time, over a period of weeks beginning in mid-September. It is a fresh-eating apple and also a good keeper. A small to medium yellow apple with thick, translucent skin and a blush on one side, it has a taste of pear to it. It came from Pennsylvania in the 1840s.

The Lowland Raspberry is a medium yellow apple with light crimson marbling. It is of Russian origin and is a hardy, sweet-tasting dessert apple. It's also known as the Liveland Raspberry and gets its name from the former Livland (or Livonia) province of Russia, which is now Lithuania. The flesh is pure white and very soft. The apple collector Lee Calhoun has described the taste of the tender flesh as "almost like eating foam."[21] It is an early ripening apple.

The final variety of apple in Frost's Ripton orchard was the Porter. This is another New England yellow apple, medium-sized, sometimes with a blush or russet on one side. The flesh is yellow and sweet, and the midseason apple ripens in September and is good for both eating fresh and cooking. It was a favourite of the cookbook author Fanny Farmer because it holds its shape when cooked.

Frost's Ripton orchard was a mix of early and midseason apples for both eating fresh and cooking. Most of the varieties were popular apples of the time.

There weren't many keepers, which suggests that Frost preferred to eat the apples fresh from the tree or transformed into jelly or sauce, rather than storing them through a long Vermont winter. (He wouldn't have been there to eat them anyway, as he wintered in Cambridge.)

Frost's apples were also all yellow.

I had thought that planting the Ripton orchard was an optimistic gesture on Frost's part, since the trees were grafted in his eighty-third year and wouldn't produce right away, making it unlikely he would be around to taste the fruit. "Too bad a first harvest can't be looked for sooner," he wrote to Fred Abbey of Gardenside Nurseries.[22] But here I have to say it was a mistake for me to believe that because I understand what it is to be a writer— and to have a close and poignant friendship with another writer, and to have a feeling for apples—I understand the man. I thought it was optimistic of Frost to plant an orchard when he was an old man close to death, because I am an optimistic person and could imagine doing that myself. But Frost wrote in one of his notebooks about planting the orchard as a way to reach forward into the future, so that his life stretched back into his past but also forward into a future he would never witness. He called it "the longing for extension in both ways."[23]

But of course, the apple trees were more than just the ego of the man who planted them. They were also practical because they produced food, and this can never be underestimated. And the little grove of yellow apples was perhaps also a memorial to the halcyon English walks with Edward Thomas, and to the memory of that important friendship. Robert Frost had both a practical and a romantic relationship with apples. They were there to eat and generate a living, but they were also there to dream on and to write poems about and for. In a handwritten letter to Ira Glackens when he was deciding what trees to plant, he confesses, "There's nothing I like to think about more than apple trees."[24]

My trip to visit the orchards doesn't include the farmhouse in Derry, New Hampshire, where Frost wrote, or was inspired to write, many of his apple poems. That orchard was severed from the farm during the tenancy of one of the subsequent owners and is now inaccessible. And more importantly, it was not planted by Robert Frost, so the apples that grew there were not his choices.

I am most interested in the Ripton orchard, but I also go and visit Frost's farm in Shaftsbury, now a museum, because there is a plan to reproduce his orchard with heritage trees in a field behind the parking lot. But again, I am less interested in this orchard because it was conceived as a commercial enterprise and the trees he chose were the standard orchard trees of the day. The first orchard already existed when he got to Derry. The second was conceived as a cash crop. But the third orchard he planted for himself, and the afterlife of those apples is in effect, as he stated in his notebooks, his own afterlife.

Ripton is a tiny Vermont village with a population of less than a thousand people. It is famous now for being the site of Robert Frost's summer habitation, and also for the renowned Bread Loaf Writers' Conference, which takes place every summer a few minutes up the road from Frost's old farmhouse. Robert Frost was instrumental in getting the first conference running, and he was an active part of it for forty-two years. Middlebury College, which runs Bread Loaf, now owns his farmhouse and writing cabin.

Ripton is uphill from the highway, at the top of a winding road with a boulder-strewn river running beside it. On the summer day when I was there, children were swimming in the river at the bridge just below the town, darting across the road with bare feet and towels around their waists.

The Frost farmhouse is white clapboard and sits at the front of the 150-acre property; it's flanked by fields, and a single apple tree stands near the house. When Frost bought the place in 1938, he rented it to friends of his, who acted as unofficial caretakers of the property during the summer months. The couple, Ted and Kay Morrison, were also intimately connected to Frost—he began a relationship with Kay after his wife's death, and Ted (who remained married to Kay throughout the affair, which lasted, in some capacity, until Frost's own death in 1963) was a poetry lecturer at Bread Loaf. The much younger Kay also became Frost's de facto secretary and helped to manage his increasing public obligations.

Frost inhabited the writing cabin only during the summer and fall months, and frequently came down to the farmhouse in the evenings to have supper with Ted and Kay. The cabin is situated behind the farmhouse and is a short walk up a gently rising hill. It is made of logs and has a screened porch on the western side. The front of the cabin, the eastern side, looks into the woods that surround the property. The small orchard was planted forty or fifty feet from the building, in the direction of the farmhouse, and would have operated as a screen, so that if someone was looking uphill, the small wooden cabin would be obscured by the trees.

Unlike the Shaftsbury farmhouse, which has ceded to its present-day museum persona, with that narrative effectively draped on top of whatever scrap of reality still exists from Frost's tenure, the writing cabin in Ripton and its surrounds are wholly unchanged, so that it feels very much as though the writer has just stepped out for a walk in the woods and will be back shortly.

I understand writers' spaces, having occupied a great number myself over the course of my life. The Ripton cabin is a very good writer's space. It is well separated from the farmhouse down the hill. The screened porch offers the outside air without the insects that inhabit it (on the July day I was there, the deerflies were numerous). The views—over the fields and to the mountains beyond on one side of the cabin, and into the woods on the other side— are spectacular and enticing. There are many writers who advocate for looking at nothing but a blank wall, to stimulate the imagination, but I have always preferred a view myself—partly because writing involves a lot of not writing and it's nice to look at something pleasant, but also because sometimes what's outside makes its way onto the page, and that blend of the real world and the imagined one is potent.

Of the twenty apple trees in Frost's original Ripton orchard, seven remain. They are relatively healthy, although some have split trunks and fungus and lichen on the branches. But they all have an abundance of apples. There is also tall grass in the orchard, full of dropped tree limbs and rocks. The rocks are numerous and I wonder if there was once a low wall in front of the orchard. At the western edge of the cluster of trees are several soft fruit canes—blackberries and raspberries just beginning to ripen.

Near to the screened cabin porch there is a large rock that makes a perfect seat and offers a great view of the orchard, with enough distance that it doesn't disturb the birds if you sit there. Also, the rock has a shallow depression in the top and fits naturally to a body, making it seem as though people have sat there for a very long time.

It was a sunny day in early July when I came to the Ripton farm. I sat on the rock outside Frost's writing cabin and listened to the whir of the poplar leaves at the edge of the woods and the sweet song of a hermit thrush. The tall grasses at the base of the apple trees were rich with wildflowers—pale yellow foxgloves, clover, flax, Indian paintbrush, Queen Anne's lace, daisies and buttercups. A robin perched in the branches of a tree above a cluster of small green apples.

It was more powerful than I had imagined, finding Frost's last orchard still thriving, the trees with fruit on them. Everything was so alive in that little spot and I was struck by the continuum of life, by how the birds used the orchard as they probably always had, by how the apples reappeared summer after summer. It was all praise and all miracle. Edward Thomas was right about a line of apples being the same as a line of poetry in another language. And while Frost was no longer there to tend his orchard, it persisted. And because he had thought about it as it was in that moment, with fruit on the trees and the trees in full maturity, it still contained him.

The poet may die, but the poetry continues.

The GHOST ORCHARD

No. 49715
Yellow Transparent.
E. P. Cahill.
Hancock Md

E. I. Schutt.
Nov. 30th '10.
Dec. 15 -'10.

Ellen Isham Schutt, *Malus domestica*, Yellow Transparent, 1910.

59494

"Pumpkin Sweet
M.F. Aherne,
Manhattan, Kans.

A.A. Newton.
10-8-'12
10-16-'12

Amanda Almira Newton, *Malus domestica*, Pumpkin Sweet, 1912.

79854

Canada
    Reinette,
Irwin Stout,
Millbridge
    Me.

J.A.Newton.
1-21-1915
1-26-1915

Amanda Almira Newton, *Malus domestica*, Canada Reinette, 1915.

Deborah Griscom Passmore, *Malus domestica*, St. Lawrence, 1892.

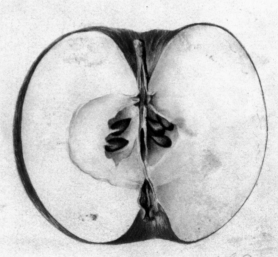

In a Canadian nursery catalogue from 1827, there are seventy-nine varieties of apple trees available to be ordered, bought and planted.[1] Some of the varieties are familiar to us today—Snow, Russet, Rhode Island Greening—but many are apples that I have never tasted and never even seen. Some have appealingly descriptive names (Monstrous Pippin, Mammoth Apple, Winter Blush), and some names seem to have changed—an apple called Yellow Harvest in the catalogue appears to exactly match one we now call the Yellow Transparent.

The local aspect of the apples is highlighted. The

catalogue is not a scientific document, but rather the transcription of a conversation between apple growers and apple sellers. Three of the varieties in the catalogue—Large Fair Soft & White, Large Green Streaked and Large Green Sweet—were named by the author, with an explanatory note to say that the apples "are very fine fruits from Mr. Cooper's famous Orchard, not having the proper names at present I have given this description."[2]

The apples are listed in the catalogue first by number, for easy reference, then by name, and then by the time of year at which they ripen. They range from early to very late keepers—the Tewksbury Winter Blush is described as keeping from October right through June, for example. The Pennock's Large Red Winter ripens in November and then keeps straight through to April. The number each apple is given corresponds to the time at which it ripens (the early numbers signify early ripening apples and so forth). The White Winter Pearmain is fiftieth out of the seventy-nine listed apples, roughly two-thirds of the way through, meaning that in 1827 it was considered an early winter apple. Three of the later apples—the Green Everlasting, Red Everlasting and Millar's Long Keeping—are said to remain edible for a full year.[3]

If you wanted to eat and cook apples right through a calendar year in 1827, you needed to be able to grow those apples yourself (or buy them locally). Fruit did not readily cross borders, as it does today, and it wasn't available out of season. An orchard in the early nineteenth century was not often a large enterprise, but it was a comprehensive one, in that it produced ripe apples from July through November. And the apples that were ripe in November, the winter apples, could be stored until spring or summer.

The orchard at Prime Minister John A. Macdonald's former house (now a museum) in Kingston is a good example of a nineteenth-century home orchard. Bellevue House was originally constructed around 1840 for a wealthy Kingston merchant. The Macdonalds rented it from him in 1848–49, a sorrowful year that included the death of their

young son, John Alexander Jr., when he was just a
year old.

Bellevue House was designed and built in the
Italianate style.[4] This meant that there were two
wings extending from a central tower in an L-shape,
and that there were different sizes and shapes to the
windows, a mix of peaked and flat roofs, and numerous small balconies. The house has just three floors,
but there are seven levels.

The Italianate style is a picturesque design, and
this design extends to the gardens. A picturesque
design is that heady mix of order and chaos—the
contained grandeur of the house juxtaposed with
a wild apple orchard full of long grass and with no
regularity to the placement of the trees. It was meant
as a status symbol. The orchard shielded the house
from the road and gave the appearance of country
living in the city.

The original orchard at Bellevue is long gone,
and a replacement orchard was planted on the site
in the 1980s. The varieties of trees in the original
orchard have been lost to the historical record, but

those that have been replanted are trees that were popular at the time, and so the chance is good that there has been overlap between the two orchards. Also, while Bellevue House is a good deal grander than most middle-class Canadian homes of the period, many of those home orchards would have included some of the same trees.

The apple trees in the modern-day Bellevue House orchard are as follows:

Baldwin: The Baldwin has an interesting nomenclature. It was first discovered on a farm in Lowell, Massachusetts, in 1740. This farm was purchased by a Mr. Butters, who decided to call the apple the Woodpecker because it was favoured by those birds. Over time, its name was shortened to the Pecker, and eventually people started calling it the Butters. The current name comes via a Colonel Baldwin, who cultivated the apple more widely and ushered in its long and prosperous commercial life. By the mid-1800s, it was a very popular apple in New England, New York and Southern Ontario. A large green-red apple with juicy yellow flesh, it ripens late, will keep right through winter, and gives reliable and generous yields.

Blood Gravenstein: This is a strain of the Gravenstein, an apple that was grown in Holland in the seventeenth century but most likely originated in Germany or Russia. It is a highly blushed, yellow-skinned apple with short, broad broken scarlet stripes. It ripens in early September and does well with cool summers, making it a popular growing apple in Nova Scotia and California. It's a good eating and cooking apple, with crisp and juicy white flesh.

Early Harvest: This apple has been mistakenly identified at Bellevue as the Summer Harvest, a variety that does not exist. The Early Harvest most likely originated in Canada in the 1700s; it ripens, as the name suggests, in July and August. Pale yellow, it has an orange blush on one side and juicy white flesh. It is used for fresh eating and for pies and sauce.

Golden Russet: Both a cider and an eating apple, with a sharp, crisp taste, the Golden Russet was propagated in the United States in the early to middle nineteenth century and would have been a fairly new apple for the original Macdonald orchard. The Golden Russet is also a good cooking apple. It is frequently confused with the English Russet, but they are different varieties (although the former probably derived as a seedling apple from the latter).

Maiden Blush: This is an early nineteenth-century American apple with pale yellow skin and a dark red blush on one side. It ripens at the beginning of September. The flesh is white, and that whiteness remains even when the apple is dried. A member of the Pennsylvania Fruit Growers' Society in the late 1800s learned that he could preserve Maiden Blush apples well into January by placing them in a basket and suspending it in a well, two feet above the water. It was an early method of apple storage that predated the root cellar and produced fruit as firm and blemish-free as the day they were picked from the tree.[5]

Northern Spy: This large red apple is renowned for being both one of the best winter apples and one of the tastiest pie apples. It ripens into November and keeps its shape and crispness all through the winter.

Pumpkin Sweet: Also known as the Pound Sweet, this is a large apple with yellowish-green skin that is often covered with a brown flush. Historically, it was used for baking, making apple butter and feeding to livestock. It ripens in September and has yellow flesh with an overly sweet taste.

Red Astrachan: This is one of the apple varieties Robert Frost planted. Not a good keeper, it is best cooked and is said to make the tastiest jelly of all the apples. It is a medium apple and yellow in colour, with streaks sometimes so numerous that it can appear to be solid red. It has Russian origins.

St. Lawrence: A distinctly Canadian variety that was discovered in Montreal in 1835, the St. Lawrence is a small green apple with red stripes; it's good for fresh eating and for making applesauce. It ripens in mid-September, but it doesn't usually last more than a month in storage.

Tolman Sweet: This was a popular tree for home orchards. The sweet yellow apple kept through winter and was good for pickling, baking, cider, drying and eating fresh. It was grown a lot in Canada and New York, and had a reputation for being hardy and a reliable producer.

Westfield Seek No Further: A medium apple from Westfield, Connecticut, it had creamy yellow skin and red stripes. It was used only as a dessert apple, which made it a bit limited, but it was also hardy and a good producer, so it was popular in the mid-nineteenth century in Ontario, New York and the American Midwest.

Winesap: This is a fairly small but uniform red apple that was once extremely popular in North America as a market apple because of its appealing taste, and because it was a good keeper. It could last almost through the winter in regular storage and right through the spring in cold storage.

Worcester Pearmain: An English apple that was popular there in the mid-nineteenth century, it was a medium red apple with a distinctive strawberry flavour. Both the apples and the blossoms were thought to be particularly attractive. It ripened in mid-September and was best eaten fresh.

The orchard at Bellevue House still functions as it did when it was planted in the 1840s. From the road, the house is completely hidden by the apple trees—even when visitors stand right up against the fence bordering the property. It seems to me that the apparently random pattern of the trees is not really random at all, but that each tree is there to plug a hole in the view and to provide passersby with a dense screen of green foliage to look at if they're trying to spy on the house. The orchard is much superior to a hedge because the staggering of the trees produces a layered effect, and unlike a hedge, the scrim of green can't simply be peered over.

Part of the appeal of the picturesque design is the unkempt "wild" appearance of the orchard, and this is maintained at Bellevue. To further the authenticity of the period, the orchard is mowed by scythe when the grass becomes too long. When I visited, the staff person on duty that day warned me about snakes—attracted, no doubt, by the tall grass, which would also be home to mice, voles, chipmunks and other animals that would enjoy feeding on the apples when they were ripe. An orchard is also very attractive to birds because of the proliferation of insects that are interested in the fruit. Like most homogenous plant groupings, orchards have their own ecosystems.

It would be remiss of me not to mention Henry David Thoreau in this book about apples, partly because of his own treatise on apple trees, but mostly because of his passion for them. I have felt a kinship with him as I tromp around this fall, eating the wild apples I discover in the fields beyond the city limits. I like his romantic declarations that wild apples should be eaten out of doors, that the conditions in which they thrive—wind and sun and rain—are also the conditions in which they should be consumed. Now we would call this "terroir," but in his day there was no name for it, just an enthusiasm: "These apples have hung in the wind and frost and rain till they have absorbed the qualities of the weather or season, and thus are highly seasoned, and they pierce and sting and permeate us with their spirit. They must be eaten in season, accordingly,—that is, out-of-doors."[6]

Thoreau also believed that one's thoughts were different outside than they were indoors, and that apples eaten outdoors tasted far superior to those that were consumed inside. One hundred and fifty-four years later, it is hard to disagree with him. There is something truly liberating about striding around the countryside (even though there is much less of it in my day than there was in his), tasting apples off different trees, throwing away the ones I don't like and knowing they will be eaten by voles and insects, that nothing will go to waste.

"All apples are good in November,"[7] declared Thoreau, and again, it's hard to find fault with that statement. An apple in November is right on the edge of winter, and the sweetness it contains seems the last little burst of summer in your mouth.

I have come to think of apple trees as akin to human beings, not just in the fact of their individuality, and their diversity, but also in the brief tenure of their lives. A hundred years is very old for an apple tree, as it is for a person. An apple tree exists for the same length of time that we do, and this gives our relationship with the trees certain poignancy.

To stand under an apple tree in May is to feel its life as the branches vibrate with the industry of bees visiting the blossoms. The noise of the bees and the rich, sweet scent of the blossoms is an intoxicating combination, and I feel, pausing at the base of the tree and looking up into the branches, that I am in the presence of the divine. The over-lapping hum of the bees is almost choral, and it's in G, which is the key of the *Goldberg Variations* and was called, in the baroque period, "the key of benediction."[8]

An apple tree in September or October is equally alive, full of birds and squirrels and insects, all intent on feeding from the ripened fruit, hanging with such poise from the upturned branches. In the fall I went "scrumping" for apples in the fields and woods around the small town where I live. ("Scrumping" is a nineteenth-century term, meaning to take the windfalls or the apples that remain on a tree after the harvest. Its meaning has been extended to include the act of stealing apples from someone else's orchard.)[9] I stayed within walking distance of town, to see what varieties still remained on the "wild" apple trees that decorated hill and heath.

I sometimes went with a friend, and I always took the dog, who enjoyed hunting mice and voles in the long grass at the base of the apple trees. I tried to stop her—not from hunting but from killing—but I was only moderately successful in this as I was often preoccupied with plucking a choice apple from high in the branches with my apple-picking "tool," which strongly resembled a lacrosse stick.

I was able to find, identify and eat—all within walking distance of my house—the following varieties of apples: Yellow Transparent, Baldwin, St. Lawrence, Jersey Mac, Winesap, Red Delicious, Snow, Gravenstein, Reinette. The Reinette was my favourite of these, and the best tasting. It also had one of the longest seasons. I was eating apples from that tree on December 5, and at the end of January I still had several in my fridge that remained edible.

All these trees were once part of orchards or kitchen gardens that have long since disappeared. Probably they survived because people were reluctant to cut them down—the trees were "useful," in that they produced food. Now they exist in little strips of wilderness between the suburbs and the city, dropping a mantle of colour onto the dry grass in the fall; they provide food for birds and mice, foxes and the odd deer that ranges through the margin of field between the fences. The apple trees, like the animals, are a reminder that the landscape was once different, with different priorities in play.

My friend died. Then, unexpectedly, my father died. All fall I walked from tree to tree, often at sunset, collecting and eating apples while the sky blazed orange or pink above the water and I thought about their deaths. Sometimes, on the way back to the car with a bag of apples in one hand and the apple-picker resting on my shoulder, I would turn to call for the dog, who was nosing in the shadows, and I would see the trees behind me, the apples glowing with the last of the sun, like lanterns on the crest of the hill.

My father had always liked trees. His father, who died in the Second World War, had wanted to move from England to Traill, BC, to start a fruit farm. My father planted a peach tree once, buying it from the nursery across the road from his house and tending it carefully through several seasons. He was excited when it bore fruit, and saddened when it succumbed to disease and eventually perished.

My father wasn't religious. He believed that we are all energy, and that our energy, when we die, is absorbed by other energies. He hoped that when he died, he would become part of a tree.

My friend Joanne, in her last days, said, "I will always be there." Meaning that to bring her back for myself, I just had to think of her. She would always be there for me. She would just stop being there for herself. And this is true and not true—the absence recalling the presence—like the apple trees on the hill, a reminder of what once was and yet persisting, still existing on their own.

Memory becomes its own ghost orchard.

There should be a word for how the dead continue and don't continue, for how the fact of them gives over to the thought of them.

Even love. Even rain. The fox crossing the leafy avenue. Darkness lifting from the field. The wet ring on the table under the beer glass. The scent of lilacs on the hill. Even laughter. Even breath won't remember you.

Nevertheless, you are still there. In the line of morning song outside the window. The dark plum of dusk. The dream. In the scatter of words on a page. The rise of green before the wild orchard.

In the taste of this apple.

The IMAGINED DISCOVERY *of the* WHITE WINTER PEARMAIN

The White Winter Pearmain, whose history I have been loosely tracing in this book, had its origins in thirteenth-century Britain. All accounts say that the apple was simply "discovered," with no explanation given as to how and by whom. The fact of the apple remained the important thing, not the story surrounding its birth—especially as that story would have had to endure for hundreds of years.

It could have been a farmer who originally found the apple. Or a traveller. Or quite possibly an animal in the company of a human. It was most likely a fairly ordinary discovery and perhaps not much was made of it. The world was much newer then. There were many discoveries. But because I have been thinking hard about the White Winter Pearmain for well over two years now, and because I want to fill in the history of this apple, to leave this account complete, I am giving you the following story as a possibility of how it could have been discovered. What follows is fiction, not fact. Not that it *did* happen this way, but that it *could have* happened this way.

I hope you will consider the story a windfall.

England, AD 1200

Sir Godfrey was riding through the countryside, enjoying the warmth of the sun on his face and the backs of his hands where they held the horse's reins. He could even feel the heat of the sun warming the metal and penetrating the tiny holes in the chain mail covering his head.

The morning was beautifully still, the only sound the lilt of birdsong and the rhythmic tap of the horse's hooves on the hard earth of the lane. Sir Godfrey was in the last stages of the long journey from Normandy, where he had left his dead ruler, King Richard, and was now on his way to present himself to Richard's brother, the newly minted King John.

King Richard had been a knight also, and he and Godfrey had fought in the Crusades together, so it was with a heavy heart that Godfrey was returning to Britain. He was not eager to meet or serve King John, so he was not hurrying along the road. In fact, he was letting his horse do whatever it wanted— walk slowly, stop when it saw a tasty clump of grass, rub its flanks against a tree trunk to satisfy an itch. Sir Godfrey and the horse had been through many battles together. They were often of one mind.

As he and the horse rounded a bend, Godfrey saw another knight and another horse ahead of him in the lane. This knight also had his helmet off, and he was not riding his horse but walking beside it.

"Hail!" called Godfrey as he rode up alongside the other man.

The knight turned in the road, and Godfrey saw that it was his friend Nicholas. This was astonishing to him for many reasons, but mostly because he had believed his friend to be dead.

"Nicholas!" he cried. "I thought you were killed at Courcelles! Sir Ralf saw your head upon a spike on the castle wall."

"That," said Nicholas, "was Adelard. But you're the second knight to have mistaken us. I don't think I look at all like Adelard. His eyes are much closer together, and his hair is the colour of mouldy straw."

"I mourned you," said Godfrey, dismounting stiffly to walk beside his friend. His back was still bothering him. It must have been from that twist in full armour to avoid the Frenchman's lance. Curse him! "I shed tears and drank myself senseless, vowed to name my next child after you."

"Did you really?" Nicholas draped an arm around his friend's shoulders. "I am moved by your sentiment."

"Well, perhaps it's not all true," admitted Godfrey.

"I did drink myself senseless, however. And I did truly lament your death. Why are you walking, not riding?"

"My horse is lame. He has a burdock lodged under his hoof. And he needs watering. I was looking for a spot to stop and tend to him."

"You're not racing back to Windsor either, then," said Godfrey. "The young knights are probably already there, jousting for favour with the new king."

"I'm weary of the young knights," said Nicholas. "They confuse recklessness with courage. Every word from their mouths is a boast or a challenge. In their tales, they are so heroic, always so bloody heroic. And they insist on the very latest equipment, as though that is better than experience."

"I've heard that Bartholomew even travels with his own blacksmith," said Godfrey.

"The arrogance!" exclaimed Nicholas. "But I'm down a gauntlet and my left couter has rusted out and it's hard to move my elbow and my horse lost his breastplate at Gisors. So I might envy him the blacksmith a little."

"Probably easier on the horse not to be carrying all that weight if he's lame."

Godfrey saw a pleasing twist of water over a spill of rocks. "There's a beck up ahead. Let's stop there."

The knights let their horses drink their fill. Then Godfrey held the head of Nicholas's horse while his friend removed the thistle spur from under its hoof. It was hot by the stream, which rested in the shelter of low-lying hills, and there was no stir of breeze in the valley. The possibility of encountering an enemy here seemed remote.

"I'm going to take off my armour," said Godfrey. "My back hurts, and I would dearly like to wash. It's been weeks since I have seen my own flesh."

"I suppose if we keep our swords to the ready." Nicholas was slightly less convinced.

They slowly removed their tunics and chain mail, then pulled the tight-fitting doublets over their heads until they were in their linen underclothes. They removed these last garments at the edge of the stream and splashed through the water like boys. The clear sky and the heat of the sun made it seem like midsummer, but the coldness of the stream told the truth of the season, that it was the middle of autumn.

Washing was brief.

Godfrey and Nicholas dressed again in their underclothes and sat with their backs against a tree, warming up in the sun and delaying the moment when they had to once again don their weighty chain mail.

"Does your sword get heavier every year?" asked Godfrey, putting his hands behind his head and closing his eyes in the strong sunshine.

"Worse than the weakness is the tiredness," said Nicholas. "I could happily sleep from midday right through to the next morning. And that is not even on a day with a battle in it."

"Perhaps the new king won't want us," said Godfrey. He opened his eyes and saw, above his head, hundreds of small yellow suns—a whole tree full of yellow apples. He reached for his sword and used it to knock several from the branches, so that they fell near enough for him to grab.

"We could take our leave," said Nicholas. "We

both have land, families who love us. Estates to govern."

"You should taste this," said Godfrey, offering one of the apples to his friend.

"But sometimes the new kings want the old knights to remain. And we could always be called back into service, even if we did leave." Nicholas took the apple but didn't bite into it.

The horses heard the crunch of an apple being eaten and ambled towards the men and the tree. Godfrey knocked some more of the yellow fruit down for them. Some of the apples had a faint blush on one side—the side nearest to the sun, perhaps.

"The trouble with farming," said Nicholas, "is that it seems appealing in the midst of battle, but it might prove tedious in practice."

"Taste the apple," said Godfrey. "I've already eaten two. There's a sweetness to the flesh that is heavenly."

"And one's family is more dear when distant, I fear. The last time I was with my wife, we had a terrible argument about her stew. I don't think we have made peace even now."

"Nicholas! Just eat the apple."

His friend at last took a bite of the yellow fruit.

"What do you think?" asked Godfrey.

"Delicious."

"Honey or nectar?"

Nicholas took another bite, considered for a moment. "Pear," he said. "I think the taste is pear. What an extraordinary thing to eat an apple that tastes like a pear."

"It's an extraordinary day, isn't it?" said Godfrey. "You have returned from the dead. We have bathed and rested and dined on an apple sweeter than any we have tasted before. We are fortunate men."

"None more so," agreed Nicholas, tossing his apple core towards the stream and watching it arc over the horses. "Let us stay here all day, my friend. We can ride to Windsor tomorrow. No one will miss us if we delay our arrival by one day."

"Daring," said Godfrey.

"Sadly, I'm more daring at rest than in battle," said Nicholas. "Pass me another of those apples, will you?"

They munched in silence for a few moments. The sun and the quiet were making Godfrey drowsy. He shook his head to clear it, but in another minute, it was sinking towards his chest again.

"If I had a short nap," he said, "would you watch over us?"

"Of course." Nicholas laid his sword across his knees and reached for another apple. "This fruit is a visitation from the divine. Do you remember that story about those souls who are conceived in orchards, and how their breath is always sweet, and that is how they recognize each other—from the apple scent on their breath? Did you ever hear that story, Godfrey? It is one of my favourites. I often think about it. Do you know it? I feel that we might have been conceived in an orchard."

He turned to his friend, but Godfrey was asleep, his head lolling on his chest, one hand still holding tightly to a yellow apple.

A GLOSSARY of LOST APPLES

T he following is a selected glossary of apples that used to exist in North America but are now extinct. I have tried to choose those whose names will convey some history and tell something of both the apple and the person who named it.

I have listed, where it was known, the first date when a particular apple was mentioned in a nursery catalogue. This is not the date of origin but merely the date of first documentation for commercial purposes. Also, apples are described in particular, standardized ways, which is why the wording in my entries is repetitive. And finally, *early season* means the summer months, *midseason* is September to mid-October, *late season* is mid-October to mid-November, and *very late season* is anything after the middle of November. Winter apples can ripen anywhere from December to April.

The number of apples in North America was once vast and practically unknowable. New varieties were discovered or invented all the time. This list is but a sampling of what existed. It is a glimpse of some of the more interesting, unusual, common-sense or puzzling varieties. It is a very small piece of a whole that is lost to us now, and for which I mourn.

Where possible, I have highlighted the apple varieties of First Nations or Canadian origin.

Adam and Eve: A medium yellow Ontario apple from 1890 with red stripes and juicy, tender yellow-and-white flesh of good quality. The apple was late season and the fruit was often "doubles," meaning two apples were commonly fused together as one.

Agathe: A late-season apple, originally from Holland, with an oblong to conical shape and of medium to large size. The Agathe had red skin with tender and juicy yellow-and-white flesh.

Anglo-American: An Ontario apple from 1854 of medium size with an oblate shape and yellow skin with red stripes. The flesh was white, tender and juicy, with very good flavour. It was a midseason apple, and the tree was hardy and productive.

Anti-Know-Nothing: All that is known of this apple is that it was from 1856 and is listed in the horticulture catalogue as being "Of Political Significance." It was probably named in defiance of the Know-Nothing Party, a US political party founded in 1849, whose members were opposed to Catholics and immigrants.

Arnold's Cheese: A summer apple listed in a Virginia nursery catalogue in 1894.

Aunt Hannah: A ribbed, oblong apple of medium to large size from Massachusetts. The skin was yellow with russet patches, and the flesh was fine and yellow with a mild sub-acid flavour. The apple was late season.

Bachelor Blush: A New Jersey apple from 1864 that was large and oblong. A yellow apple, it had a blush on one side. The white flesh was tender, crisp and juicy, and the quality was very good. It was an early to midseason apple.

Batingme: Listed in an 1897 catalogue from Kentucky, this apple was described as "the largest we have ever seen."[1] It was a bright red apple with white flesh that ripened towards the end of July.

Bird Seedling: Found in a 1916 catalogue from Arkansas, this apple had no description attached to the provocative name.

Black Michigan: A Canadian apple of medium size with an oblate shape. It was a red-striped apple and was late season.

Bloomless and Coreless: Described as a "curiosity only," this apple was from Virginia and had yellow, green and red skin. The quality of the apple was good, and it ripened late season.

British Columbia: A medium to large Canadian apple with yellow skin and russet patches. It was late season and the quality was described as very good.

Bushwhacker: A round to conical apple from New Jersey of large size and with yellow skin. The apple was of good quality and ripened very late in the season.

Byson: An English russet apple of small to medium size with a crisp and juicy greenish flesh. A dessert apple of good quality, it was ready late season. Also known as Byson's Wood and Byson's Wood Russet.

Calumet: A Quebec apple from 1893 that was described as both round and oblong, and of both medium and large size. It was a greenish-yellow apple with red stripes and fine, juicy white flesh. It was of good quality and was ripe in late season.

Catface: A large Kentucky late-season apple of oblong to conical shape with red-striped, greenish-yellow tender flesh. Described as a good-quality apple with brisk sub-acid flavour.

Cherokee: Also called the Cherokee Red, this very large red apple from the American South had somewhat dry, yellow flesh. It ripened very late. It was listed in gardening catalogues around the mid-nineteenth century.

Chester: A white apple with a yellow blush from Pennsylvania. It had tender and juicy white flesh with a pleasant taste and was medium-sized and of oblong shape. It was a midseason apple.

Cons: Another white apple, this one had red stripes and came from Pennsylvania. The white flesh was tender and juicy, and the quality was good to very good. It was listed as a dessert apple.

Craven's Winter: A small yellow apple with russet patches from Kentucky. It was mentioned in nursery catalogues in 1870. The flavour was described as sweet and good.

Delaware Bottom: A Maryland apple from before 1868 that was primarily used for cooking. It was oblate in shape, with yellow skin with a blush, and was late ripening.

Democrat: A New York apple from 1853, medium to large in size and round in shape. It was listed as white, yellow, red and crimson in colour, and had tender and juicy white-stained flesh. The quality was very good, and it was a late-season apple.

Dobbin's Everbearing: A striped South Carolina apple from 1878, medium to large in size. It was ripe from the beginning of May to the beginning of August.

Dumpling: Also known as Crooked Limb, Crooked Limb Pippin, French Pippin, Watrous Dumpling and Watson's Dumpling, this Belgian apple from 1853 was oblate and very large. It was yellow with red stripes and had tender yellow-white flesh. It was a late apple.

Durable: Also known as Durable Keeper, this large, round red-striped apple from Indiana was listed in the nursery catalogues in 1861. It was of good quality and ripened very late in the season.

Eardrop: Also known as Ladies' Ear Drop, this was an oblong yellow apple from New York with a blush. Medium in size, it had good flavour and ripened late in the season. Described as "a beautiful lemon yellow, with a brilliant scarlet cheek," and as "an ornamental fruit for the table . . . not surpassed in beauty of appearance."[2]

Early Breakfast: A large, red-striped Indiana apple, listed in the catalogues in 1891, this variety had an oblate shape and tender flesh, and was of very good quality. As the name implies, it was an early season apple.

Edith: A Canadian apple of medium to large size, listed in 1886, it was yellow with red stripes and fine yellow flesh, and was used as a kitchen and dessert apple.

Enormous: A Russian apple from Vermont in 1879 that was very large and had red-striped flesh. It ripened midseason and it was noted for its poor-quality fruit.

Eureka: A Wisconsin apple from 1900, round to oblate and large in size. It was pale yellow with red and scarlet on its skin, and it had fine, mild and juicy white flesh that was sweet and very good in flavour. It ripened very late in the season.

Fail-Never: Also known as Fail-Me-Never and Neverfail, this Scottish apple was oblate in shape and medium to large in size. It had dark red skin with a sweet taste and was of good quality. It was used as a kitchen apple and ripened late.

Ferris Wheel: An oblate to conical, medium-sized apple from Iowa that was listed in catalogues in 1876. It was yellow-skinned with crimson patches, and had white, sweet flesh of good quality. It was a midseason apple.

Fisher: A very large apple from 1852 with a very late season, it was described as "a handsome long keeper."[3]

Frazier's Hard Skin: An apple from Greensboro, North Carolina, that was listed in the nursery catalogues there from 1893 to 1895.

Frogmore: Also known as Frogmore Nonpareil and Frogmore Prolific, this was a large green apple with blush and fine, crisp and juicy white flesh. A kitchen apple, it had an early to mid-autumn ripening season.

Front Door: A West Virginia apple with an oblate shape and of medium to large size. It was a yellow apple with red stripes and tender, juicy white flesh. The quality was described as good, and it was primarily used as a dessert apple. The ripening season was early to mid-autumn.

Glass: A Russian apple, listed in the catalogues in 1886, it was oblong to oblate in shape, with a yellow blushed skin. The flesh was fine and white, and the quality was very good.

Goff: This apple from Ohio was listed in 1856. It was medium to large in size, oblate in shape and pure white in colour. The flesh was fine and tender and also white, and the taste was brisk and sub-acid. It was a kitchen and market apple, and ripened in early to midseason.

Golden Wilding: Used by Thomas Jefferson in his Monticello orchard to make cider in 1796, this round to oblate apple with gold skin had a profusion of brown dots on it. The flesh was yellow and fine, and the apple ripened as late as December.

Gooseberry: A large apple from England, with a round to conical shape. The skin was green with a yellow blush, and it had yellow flesh that was crisp, tender and juicy. The quality was good, and the apple was used as a kitchen apple and ripened in late season.

Granny Spice: A medium round apple with yellow skin that was listed in 1845. It had very good sub-acid flavour and ripened early.

Great Bearer: A Pennsylvania apple listed in 1894, with an oblate to conical shape and yellow skin with red stripes. The yellow flesh had a texture that was fine, tender and juicy, and a good flavour that was mild sub-acid. The apple was a late-season market and cider apple.

Great Keeper: An oblate russet apple with a sub-acid flavour and a very late ripening time.

Great Unknown: An apple that was brought forward by Silas McDowell of North Carolina in the middle to late 1800s. It was named the Great Unknown because he didn't know where it had come from or who gave it to him. It was a large, round to oblate yellow apple with red marbling. The yellow flesh was very tender, and the apple ripened in midseason.

Guerin: A Quebec apple listed in 1896, it was large and had greenish-yellow skin with red stripes. The white flesh was fine and juicy, and the quality was very good. It ripened midseason.

Hazel: From a catalogue of 1838, where the only description is that the apple is "possibly a pear."[4]

Henhouse: A yellow apple with tender flesh of a pleasant quality and a good taste. It was listed in an 1880 catalogue.

Hoary Morning: A large English apple of oblate to conical shape and with red-striped yellow skin. The white flesh was fine, with a brisk sub-acid taste, and the quality was good. This was a kitchen apple and ripened midseason.

Hog Snout: A medium to large North Carolina apple that was red-striped, had good flavour and was late season.

Hornet: A large, yellow Pennsylvania apple of good flavour.

Indiahoma: This Texas variety was described in a nursery catalogue from 1920 as having "originated in the old Indian Territory. Large, oblong, of excellent flavor; red. Well adapted to southwestern planting. Ripe in July. Trade-marked."[5]

Indian Winter: A southern yellow apple with sub-acid flavour and good quality. It had a very late season.

Iron: A large, oblate green apple with yellow blush from Nova Scotia. The yellow-white flesh was fine and juicy, and the quality was good to very good. It was a late-season apple.

Jane: This Pennsylvania apple with yellow blush and of medium size was listed in 1856. The yellow flesh was crisp and juicy, with a mild sub-acid flavour. Quality was good and the apple was late season.

Jessup: Also known as Jessup's Seedling and listed in an Indiana catalogue in 1866, but with no further description. There is some possibility that it originally derived from Ann Jessop.

Jiles: A winter apple of medium size that was "a great favorite in Tidewater, Virginia"[6] in the early nineteenth century.

Jones Cider: A North Carolina apple, listed from 1877, it was said to "make the finest cider, keeping sweet through the entire winter."[7]

Keep Forever: A Tennessee apple that was listed in 1860.

Kitchen: An Ohio apple with yellow skin and of medium to large size. It had good flavour and was late season.

Kittageskee: This was a Cherokee apple from North Carolina and Georgia. It was a small, bright yellow apple that had excellent flavour. It was a prolific bearer, late season and late keeper. Trees were sent to France in 1860, and according to S. A. Beach, the apple was still being produced in France up until the Second World War.

La Salle: A Canadian apple, listed in 1901, it was greenish-yellow with red stripes and an oblong to conical shape.

Large White Sweet: A North Carolina apple, listed in 1855. Ripe in August.

Ledge: An apple from New Hampshire, of medium size and oblate shape. It was a whitish-yellow colour with red stripes, and the yellow flesh was tender, juicy and mild. The taste was sweet and the quality was good to very good. Used as a kitchen apple, it was late season.

Lopside: An Ohio apple of medium to large size and covered with red stripes. It was oblate in shape and had good flavour. A late-season apple.

Lorne: Also known as the Marquis of Lorne, this apple was from Nova Scotia and was large to very large in size and round to oblate in shape. It was whitish-yellow with red stripes and had white flesh that was described as crisp, tender and juicy. It had a brisk sub-acid flavour and the quality was good to very good. A midseason apple.

Lucy Red: Also known as Lucy's Red Cheek, this was a California apple of round to oblate shape and of medium to large size. It was red-striped and ripened early to midseason.

Mamma: Also known as the Mammy Apple, this southern variety was of oblate shape and medium to large size, with yellow flesh of rich sub-acid flavour. It was a midseason apple.

Maple: An Iowa apple that was medium-sized and oblate in shape. It was yellow with a sweet flavour and of very good quality. It ripened early in the season.

Marsh: This apple was grown from a seed of the Buff apple (an old Cherokee apple) in Tennessee in 1876. It was a round green apple with red stripes. The flesh was greenish-white, very juicy and tender. The apple ripened in winter.

McAfee: A Kentucky apple, also known as Gray Apple, Gray's Keeper, Hubbardston, Indian, Indian Ladies' Favorite, Large Striped Pearmain, Large

Striped Winter Pearmain, McAfee Missourian, McAfee's Nonsuch, McAfee's Red, Missouri Keeper, Missouri Superior, New Missouri Nonsuch, Park, Park Keeper, Russian Snorter, Stephenson, Storr's Wine, Striped Pearmain, Striped Sweet Pippin, Striped Winter Pearmain, Uncle Zeeke, Valandigham Wine, White Crow, White Pearmain, Wyandotte and Zeeke. No other apple besides the Nickajack has more names than this, which says much about its popularity over a period of time. This large apple was round to oblate to conical in shape and had yellow, green, red-striped and crimson skin. The yellow-white flesh was tender and crisp, the flavour mild sub-acid and the quality good to very good. It was a dessert and market apple, and was midseason to late season.

Miller Cherokee: Also known as Miller's Cherokee, this was a large Utah apple with a very late season.

Montreal Peach: A Quebec apple that was also known as Peach of Montreal, it had an oblong to conical shape, was medium to large in size and had yellow skin. The flavour was sub-acid and the quality was very good. It was a dessert and market apple and ripened midseason.

Mount Gilead: An Ohio apple that was reported to have been planted by Johnny Appleseed, it was medium in size and had yellow-red skin. The taste was sub-acid and the season was late.

Muscat: Also known as Muscat Reinette, this was a medium-sized German apple with red-striped yellow skin and juicy yellow-white flesh. It had a rich sub-acid flavour and was midseason to late season.

Nantahalee: This apple was named by the pomologist Jarvis Van Buren, but it was found before 1855 on "an old Indian farm"[8] in Alabama. It was medium to large in size, oblate to conical in shape and had yellowish-green skin. The white flesh was tender and juicy, and the apple ripened early.

Nova Scotian: This apple was listed in catalogues in 1877 as being from, as the name suggested, Nova Scotia. It was round to oblate to conical in shape and was a large yellow apple with red stripes. The yellow-white flesh was tender and juicy, with sub-acid flavour. The quality was very good to best, and it was a late-season apple. (Rarely was an apple described as "best" in terms of quality, so this must have been a very good apple indeed.)

November: Listed in 1855, this North Carolina apple ripened in November.

Nutmeg: A red-striped Indiana apple of very good quality that ripened midseason.

Oneida: Also known as Oneida Chief, this was a New York State apple.

Ontario: As the name suggests, this apple came from Ontario and was oblate to conical in shape, large in size and had a whitish-yellow skin with red stripes on it. The white-yellow flesh was fine, tender and juicy, and the flavour was sub-acid. The season was very late.

Oostanaula: A Tennessee apple that was found in a field in 1886, it was greenish yellow with a faint blush on one side and tender yellow flesh. It had a sweet flavour and ripened early. The apple could be used for fresh eating, cooking and drying.

O'Toole's Indian Rareripe: Listed in 1870 in Kentucky, this was a large, round to conical apple with greenish-yellow skin and a blush. The flesh was greenish white, tender and sub-acid. It was an early to mid-season apple. It was also referenced in 1874 in Kirkland, New York, as follows: "The native Indian Orchard in Stockbridge, Madison County, furnished several excellent varieties of fruit, one of the best being the summer apple, known as O'Toole's Indian Rareripe."[9]

Ox: A large Pennsylvania apple with a blushed white skin and white flesh that was crisp, tender and juicy.

The apple was of good quality and ripened mid-season to late season.

Peach Pond: Also known as Peach Pond Sweet and Peach Pound Sweet, this was a New York apple of medium size and round to oblate to conical in shape. It was red-striped and had mild, juicy flesh. The quality was very good. It was primarily a dessert and market apple that ripened midseason.

Pioneer: From Pennsylvania, California and New Zealand, this was a medium apple of round to oblate to conical shape with a greenish-yellow skin and juicy whitish-yellow flesh. The flavour was pleasant and sub-acid, and the quality was good to very good. This apple ripened midseason to late season.

Pleasegood: Also known as the Pleasegood Nonsuch, this was an Ontario apple that was round to oblate. It was large in size, with red-striped yellow skin and tender, juicy yellow flesh. It was a dessert apple of very good quality and ripened midseason.

Poorhouse: Also known as Winter Green and Winter Queen, this large Tennessee apple was round to oblate, with yellowish-green russeted skin. The yellow flesh was crisp, mild and juicy, and the flavour was sub-acid. The quality of the apple was very good, and it was late season. A single apple from this tree could weigh one and a half pounds.

Prairie Gem: An Ontario apple from 1837 that was round to oblate in shape and yellow to crimson in colour. The flesh was fine, crisp and juicy, with sub-acid flavour, and the quality of the apple was good. It was a kitchen apple. Season not specified.

Proliferous: Also known as Proliferous Reinette, this was a medium-sized English apple with juicy yellow-white flesh with a rich, brisk sub-acid flavour. It was a midseason apple.

Pucker End: A large New York apple with pale yellow skin that had a crimson blush. The yellow flesh was crisp and juicy, and the flavour was sub-acid. The apple was of good quality and ripened midseason.

Quaker: A Pennsylvania apple listed in 1856, it was medium in size and had a round to conical shape. The white flesh was crisp and juicy, and the flavour was pleasant and sub-acid. The quality was good, and the apple was primarily a market apple. It was midseason to late season.

Quebec: Also known as the Quebec Sweet and Quebec Winter Sweet, this was a medium yellow-red apple of very good quality that ripened in late season.

Red Warrior: A large Georgia apple, listed in 1871, with juicy white flesh and a very late season. It was "a native Indian seedling."[10]

Republican Pippin: A large, oblate Pennsylvania apple with red-striped yellow skin and tender, juicy white flesh. It had a pleasant sub-acid flavour. It was listed in the catalogues in 1840 as a good-quality kitchen apple that ripened midseason to late season.

Rochelle: Listed in 1894, this Quebec apple was large and round to oblate, with red-striped yellow-green skin and a late season.

Rough and Ready: This North Carolina apple was listed in 1853 as round and pale red, and it ripened very late. Another apple by the same name was listed in a 1927 South Carolina catalogue, where it was described as "the best, most prolific, late winter apple; will keep until May."[11]

Saint James: A Canadian apple that was medium to large in size and oblong in shape. It was listed in an 1886 catalogue, where it was described as having yellow-red skin with russeting and fine, tender, juicy yellow flesh. The flavour was sub-acid.

Schoolfield: An apple from either Arkansas or

Tennessee, it was listed in a catalogue in 1873 with the note that it was late season.

Seager: Also known as the Townsend and the Hocking, this was a Pennsylvania apple of First Nations origin. In the Downings' book on apples, a Charles Sitgreave, Esq., provided the following history: "The original tree grew on a tract of land owned by Indians near Lumberville, in Bucks County, Pennsylvania, and was of enormous size anterior to the Revolutionary war, when the tract was sold by the Indians, with a reservation 'that the fruit of this tree should be free to all, as it had been to them and to their fathers.'"[12] The fruit was large and round to oblate, with greenish-yellow skin that was covered in brown or red patches. The white flesh was tender and juicy, with a rich and pleasant flavour. The apple was early season.

Seneca: Also known as the Seneca Favorite, this was listed in an 1849 catalogue as being from New York.

Skeleton: An apple from Arkansas, listed in 1895, it was large and yellowish white, with red stripes and a round to conical shape. The yellow flesh was tender and juicy, and the flavour was rich and sub-acid. It was an early apple of good quality.

Stormproof: As the name suggests, this Texas tree was not easily damaged by storms. Listed in 1923, it had medium apples of a light green colour and sweet taste that kept well.

Summer Harvey: A New Brunswick apple with a round to oblate shape and a large size. It had a greenish-yellow skin with a blush, and the white flesh was tender and juicy. The flavour was brisk sub-acid, and the apple was of overall good quality. It ripened early to midseason.

Sweet Seeknofurther: A New Hampshire apple of medium to large size and with a round to conical shape. The skin was yellow and green with a blush, and the flesh was fine and juicy and sweet. The apple was good quality and ripened very late.

Ten Shillings: A medium-sized, round to oblate apple with a russet covering greenish-yellow skin. The yellow-white flesh was tender and the flavour was sub-acid. The apple was midseason.

Thinskin: Listed in a catalogue of 1896, this apple was given no description.

Tippecanoe: A large apple from Indiana with yellow skin and a blush on one side. The yellow flesh was fine, crisp and juicy, and the flavour was sub-acid. The apple was listed in 1895 and described as having good quality and ripening midseason.

Trippe's Railroad: A Georgia apple, listed from 1858 and said to have been found near a railroad track. This small apple was round with red skin and of very good quality. It was a midseason apple.

(There are often apple trees growing along rail tracks because of cores tossed from long-ago trains by long-ago passengers.)

Turn-off Lane: Also known as the Strawberry, Turn in the Lane and Winter Strawberry, this New Jersey apple was small to medium in size and oblate to conical in shape. The skin was yellow, red and scarlet, and the white flesh was tender. The apple had a brisk sub-acid flavour and was described as being of good quality. It ripened very late season.

Uncle Archy: This apple from Ohio, listed in 1846, was of medium to large size, with a round to conical shape. The skin was green with russet patches, and the yellow flesh was tender and juicy. It was of very good quality and ripened in late season.

Uncle John: Also known as Uncle Richard's Graft, this Pennsylvania oblong apple was of medium size and was white with red stripes. The white flesh was tender and juicy, and the flavour was sub-acid. The quality was good to very good, and it ripened midseason.

Underleaf: An English apple, also known as Hertfordshire Underleaf, it was large and conical with yellow skin, a sub-acid flavour and an early to midseason.

Valley: Also known as the Queen of the Valley, this Connecticut apple was medium to large in size, round to conical in shape and had yellow skin covered in red stripes. The white flesh was juicy and tender, and the flavour was pleasant sub-acid. The quality was good to very good, and the apple was midseason.

Verbena: This large Wisconsin apple, listed in 1895, was of medium size and oblate shape. The skin was yellow, red and scarlet, and the yellow flesh was fine and juicy. The flavour was sub-acid, and the quality was very good. The apple ripened in late season.

Victuals and Drink: Also known as the Big Sweet, Fall Green Sweet and Green Sweet, this large apple from New Jersey was listed in 1845 and had an oblong to conical shape and yellow skin covered with russet. The yellow flesh was tender, and the flavour was brisk, rich and sweet. It was of very good quality and was used as a dessert and kitchen apple. It ripened midseason.

Virgin Mary: Listed in Georgia in 1861 but originally from Kentucky, this yellow-white apple had sweet flesh and ripened early.

Volunteer: Also known as Wilson's Volunteer, this Ohio apple was large and round to oblate, with red-striped yellow skin and tender, juicy greenish-yellow flesh. The flavour was sub-acid and the quality was good, and it was used primarily as a kitchen apple. It was late season and described as "not fit to eat till the New Year. Must be stored in a damp place to obtain perfection, then it becomes mellow with a musky flavor."[13]

War Woman: This Georgia apple was listed in 1905 and described as medium in size with yellow skin that was covered by red marbling and large grey dots. The flesh was mild and sub-acid, and the apple was very late ripening—going from December to April.

Warren: This was a winesap seedling, listed in a Texas catalogue in 1920. It was a large, red, flavourful midseason apple that was "a favourite among southern orchardists."[14]

White Apple: This apple was from Kentucky and was described as being oblong in shape and having, oddly, yellow and not white skin. It was a late-season apple.

White Doctor: Listed in 1853, this large Pennsylvania apple had a round to oblate shape and greenish-yellow skin. The white flesh was tender, and the flavour was brisk sub-acid. The quality was good, and the apple was used for both kitchen and market. It ripened midseason.

Whitney: Also known as the Whitney Russet and Whitney's Russet, this was probably a Canadian apple, of small size and an oblate to conical shape. It was yellow with a russet blush and tender, juicy yellow flesh. The flavour was rich sub-acid, and the quality was described as very good. The Whitney was used as a dessert apple and had a very long season.

Winter Cheese: A large, oblate Virginia apple with red stripes and sub-acid flavour, it was of good quality and was harvested late season.

Winter Rose: Listed in 1896, this Ontario apple was large and oblate, with greenish-red skin and mild, juicy white flesh of a sub-acid flavour. It was of good quality and was a late-season apple.

Witch: Also known as Lancaster Witch, it was possibly from Ohio.

Woodpile: Listed in 1895, this large apple from Tennessee was round to conical with red stripes and yellow-white skin. The flesh was yellow, tender and juicy, and the flavour was sub-acid. The quality of the apple was very good, and it ripened mid-season.

Yellow Forest: This was a wild apple, found by a soldier in Louisiana, who transplanted it from the woods to his nearby home. It was sold in Louisiana nurseries from 1887, and was used to make "cider almost as clear as water"[15] and also for drying, as the flesh did not darken when exposed to air. It was medium to large in size, round to oblate in shape, and had greenish-yellow skin and tender, juicy flesh that had a sub-acid flavour and was very aromatic. An early to midseason apple that was a good keeper.

Yellow Meadow: This southern apple was large and oblate, with a greenish-yellow skin and yellow flesh that was sub-acid in flavour. It was a good-quality apple and ripened midseason.

Young America: Listed in Virginia in 1895, this yellow apple was medium to large in size and ripened early in the summer.

Zane: Also known as the Zane Greening, this Virginia apple was listed in 1853. It was a large apple with greenish-yellow skin and greenish-white flesh that had a sub-acid flavour. It was of overall poor quality and ripened very late.

Zoar: Listed in 1895, this Ohio apple, also known as the Zoar Transparent, was of large size and was round to oblate in shape. It had white skin with red and scarlet patches, and the yellow flesh was very juicy and tender. The quality of the apple was very good, and it was used for dessert. It ripened midseason.

ACKNOWLEDGEMENTS

As always, and with ever-increasing gratitude, I would like to thank my agent, Clare Alexander.

Thanks to my editors, Jane Warren and Jennifer Lambert, for believing in this book and making it better.

Thanks to my stellar companions on the various apple research trips—Nancy Jo Cullen, Susan Mockler and Lori Vos (navigator extraordinaire!).

Thanks to Barbara Adams, Mary Louise Adams, Steve Heighton, Mary Huggard, Frances Humphreys, Jenna Johnson, Joy McBride, Eleanor MacDonald,

Kirsteen MacLeod, Marco Reiter, Merilyn Simonds, Alex Simpson, Raymond Vos and Mary Wight-Young, for apple research assistance.

Special thanks to the BDL members—Kirsteen MacLeod, Susan Olding and Sarah Tsiang. (Best group I ever joined.)

Thanks to Andrew Westoll and University of Toronto Scarborough, and to Irwin Streight and the Royal Military College of Canada, for residencies where some of this manuscript was written.

I am grateful to the Guilford College Archives, Guilford, North Carolina, and the Robert Frost Collection, Rauner Special Collections Library, at Dartmouth College in Hanover, New Hampshire, for material used in this book.

Thanks to Kris Dimnik of Bellevue House.

Thanks to Karen Osburn of the Geneva Historical Society, Geneva, New York, and to Barbara Lamb of the Geneva Fortnightly Reading Club, for their wonderful research assistance.

Thanks to Noelle Zitzer.

Lastly, I would like to thank Emily Herring Wilson for her help, her company and her continuing friendship—all of which have been the unexpected windfall of writing this book on apples.

Notes

1. Originally the word was *parmain* or *permain*, from the Middle French for "apple or pear."
2. Michael Tortorello, "An Apple a Day, for 47 Years," *New York Times*, October 22, 2014. The article references *The Illustrated History of Apples in North America* by Dan Bussey, forthcoming from JAK KAW Press.

The Indian Orchard
1. Gary Paul Nabhan, "The Fatherland of Apples," *Orion Magazine*, May 30, 2008.
2. Anita Vickers, *The New Nation* (Westport, CT: Greenwood Publishing Group, 2002), p. 113.

3. John Russell Bartlett, *Dictionary of Americanisms: A Glossary of Words and Phrases Usually Particular to the United States* (New York: Little, Brown, 1877), p. 313. It is interesting to note that the following entry is for "Indian Peaches." These are described as "ungrafted peach-trees, which are considered to be more thrifty and to bear larger fruit than the others."

4. Letter from D. W. H. Howard of Wauseon, OH, *Annual Report of the Ohio State Board of Agriculture for the Year 1889* (Columbus, OH: Board of Agriculture, 1890), p. 271.

5. Letter to the editor from E. P. Powell, *Garden and Forest,* vol. 4 (December 30, 1891).

6. J. H. French, *Gazetteer of the State of New York* (Syracuse, NY: R. Pearsall Smith, 1860), p. 495.

7. Letter from John Eliot, in James Constantine Pillig, *Bibliography of the Algonquian Languages* (Washington, DC: Government Printing Office, 1891), p. 179.

8. James C. Benner, *History of Georgia Agriculture 1732–1860* (Athens, GA: University of Georgia Press, 2009), p. 155.

9. "Bumper Crop: A History of the Apple Industry in Northwest Arkansas," from the website of the Shiloh Museum of Ozark History, http://www.shilohmuseum.org/exhibits/apples-intro.php.

10. W. W. Clayton, *History of Lafayette, New York* (Syracuse, NY: D. Mason & Co., 1878).

11. *Indian Orchard Report from Secretary of the State Horticultural Society of Michigan*, vol. 10, part 1880 (Michigan State Horticultural Society, 1881), p. 237.

12. *Annual Report of the Secretary of the State Horticultural Society of Michigan*, vol. 17, part 1887 (Michigan State Horticultural Society, 1887), p. 339.

13. Andrew H. Green, *Kanadesaga: An Historical Sketch of the Indian Landmarks of Geneva, N.Y.* (report of the American Scenic and Historic Preservation Society to the Legislature of the State of New York), (Albany, NY: J. B. Lyon Company, 1909), p. 285.

14. Frederick Cook, *Journals of the Military Expedition of Major General John Sullivan Against the Six Nations of Indians in 1779* (Auburn, NY: Knapp, Peck and Thomson, Printers, 1887), p. 336.

15. *The Journal of Lieut. John L. Hardenbergh of the Second New York Continental Regiment from May 1 to October 3, 1779, in General Sullivan's Campaign Against the Western Indians* (Auburn, NY: Knapp and Peck, Printers, 1879), pp. 82–87.

16. Cook, *Journals of John Sullivan*, p. 576.

17. Ibid.

18. Ibid., p. 46.

19. Ibid., p. 365.

20. John Riley, *The Once and Future Great Lakes Country: An Ecological History* (Montreal and Kingston: McGill-Queen's University Press, 2013), p. 67.

21. French, *Gazetteer of the State of New York*, p. 499.

22. Green, *Kanadesaga: An Historical Sketch*, p. 305.

23. Arthur Caswell Parker, *Iroquois Uses of Maize and Other Food Plants* (Albany: University of the State of New York, 1910), pp. 94–95.

24. Lewis Morgan also made a very extensive survey of the beaver, preparing a detailed map of 150 beaver dams in northern Michigan and studying the activity of those dams.

25. In a rare image of the area from 1879 in the collection of New York Heritage (https://www.nyheritage.org/), the apple trees are huge and plentiful.

26. S. A. Beach, *The Apples of New York,* vol. 1 (Albany: J. B. Lyon Company, 1905), p. 5.

27. The text that accompanies this photograph says: "Within sight of the Geneva Experiment Station are two very old Indian apple trees, the only ones in this vicinity now left out of many hundreds which the Indians were growing in the clearings about their town of Kanadesaga, which was located here. The illustration shows the present appearance of one of the trees. Both bear winter fruit of medium size. The fruit of one is very good

for cooking, that of the other is pleasant flavored, subacid and very good for eating. Neither has been propagated." Ibid., p. 6.

28. For example, the theme in 1909 was "Scotland: Its History and Romance," and among the topics discussed were Physical Scotland; History of *Macbeth*; Witchcraft and Superstition; John Knox; Mary, Queen of Scots; Clans and Tartans; Scottish Music and Ballet; Presbyterianism; Edinburgh. There are no minutes available for 1908, but seeing as they erected the burial mound marker that year, it might have been when they discussed "Indians."

29. This information was found in a letter from a former member of the Fortnightly Reading Club, sent to a friend on February 9, 1945. This letter is in the collection of the Geneva Historical Society in Geneva, New York.

30. Editorial in the *Geneva Gazette*, August 8, 1879.

31. Silas Tertius Rand, *Dictionary of the Language of the Micmac Indians: Who Reside in Nova Scotia, New Brunswick, Prince Edward Island, Cape Breton and Newfoundland* (Halifax: Nova Scotia Printing Company, 1888).

32. George Johnson and Charles Henry Lugrin, *Canada: A Memorial Volume* (Montreal: E. B. Biggar, 1889).

33. Malcolm Dunn, *Apples and Pears 1885: Report of the Apple and Pear Congress Held by the Royal Caledonian Horticultural Society, Edinburgh, from 25th to 28th November 1885* (Edinburgh: Maclachlan and Stewart, 1887).

34. *Annual Report of the Secretary of the State Pomological Society of Michigan*, vol. 18 (Lansing, MI: W. S. George & Company, 1889), p. 157.

35. *Transactions of the New York State Agricultural Society for the Year 1871* (Albany: Argus Company Printers, 1872), p. 622.

36. Creighton Lee Calhoun, Jr., *Old Southern Apples: A Comprehensive History and Description of Varieties for Collectors, Growers, and Fruit Enthusiasts* (White River Junction, VT: Chelsea Green Publishing, 2010).

37. A. J. Downing and Charles Downing, *The Fruits and Fruit Trees of America* (New York: John Wiley & Son, 1872), p. 251.

38. Letter to the editor from Silas McDowell, *Southern Cultivator*, vol. 15 (1857), p. 123.

39. This is according to research done by Tom Brown, who has tracked down many old and previously extinct varieties of North American apples. Brown's findings are available on his website, www.applesearch.org.

40. "Indian Orchard: Area Girl Scouts to 'Rough It' at New Seneca Day Camp Site," *Geneva Daily Times*, July 3, 1952.

41. Statement of purpose from the Oneida Community Integrated Food Systems in Green Bay, WI, https://oneida-nsn.gov/resources/oneida-community-integrated-food-systems/why-buy-local/.

ANN JESSOP

1. Calhoun, *Old Southern Apples*.

2. Terri L. Premo, *Winter Friends: Women Growing Old in the New Republic, 1785–1835* (Chicago: University of Illinois Press, 1990), p. 164.

3. Algie I. Newlin, *The Battle of New Garden* (Greensboro, NC: North Carolina Friends Historical Society, 1977). All details of the Battle of New Garden have been derived from Professor Newlin's account—which is the definitive source for this particular battle of the Revolutionary War.

4. Margaret Supplee Smith and Emily Herring Wilson, *North Carolina Women Making History* (Chapel Hill, NC: University of North Carolina Press, 1999), pp. 62–63.

5. Thomas Jessop, will dated November 20, 1783, in Jasper Newton Jessup, *Jessup Family: Containing a*

History of the Jessup Family in England and America (Little Rock, AK: 1908), p. 41.

6. Ibid.

7. William Wade Hinshaw and Thomas Worth Marshall, *Encyclopedia of American Quaker Genealogy*, vol. 1 (Baltimore, MD: 1938), p. 509.

8. State Horticultural Association of Pennsylvania, *A List of Apples, Pears, Peaches, Plums and Cherries* (Harrisburg, PA: Meyers Printing and Publishing House, 1889), p. 47.

9. This is according to Ann Jessop's great-great-great-great-great-great-granddaughter, Emily Herring-Wilson.

10. *Quaker Meeting Records: Minutes 1783–1800*, Guilford College Archives, Greensboro, North Carolina.

11. Jasper Newton Jessup, *Jessup Family*, p. 40.

12. These wagons were driven by four to six horses and were covered with canvas that was stretched over wooden hoops set along the wagon bed. The bed of the wagon curved up at each end so that the contents wouldn't fall out. For reasons unknown, the Conestoga wagon was named after the Conestoga people, who were essentially wiped out by the settlers.

13. Henry Griswold Jesup, *Edward Jessup of West Farms, Westchester Co., New York and His Descendants* (Cambridge, MA: John Wilson and Sons, 1887), p. 365.

14. Daniella J. Kostroun and Lisa Vollendorf, *Women, Religion, and the Atlantic World (1600–1800)* (Toronto: University of Toronto Press, 2009).

15. All information on Hannah Stephenson cited in this chapter is derived from William and Thomas Evans, *Piety Promoted: In a Collection of Dying Sayings of Many of the People Called Quakers*, vol. 2 (Philadelphia: Friends' Book Store, 1854).

16. Ibid., p. 332.

17. Addison Coffin, "Early Settlement of Friends in North Carolina: Traditions and Reminiscences" (unpublished paper written in 1894), Friends Historical Collection, Guilford College Archives, Guilford, NC, library.guilford.edu/fhc.

18. On June 22, it was ninety-one degrees in London; the entire summer was a hot one for the UK. See http://booty.org.uk/booty.weather/metindex .htm, a blog by Martin Rowley about historical British weather.

19. Coffin, "Early Settlement of Friends in North Carolina."

20. Calhoun, *Old Southern Apples*, p. 161.

21. Ibid.

22. Presumably the second *S* was left out for the sake of the effort it would have taken to carve it, given that the carving was done by hand with rudimentary tools.

23. Westfield has a Quaker connection to New Garden, and the meeting houses were linked, with Westfield literally the "western field" of the New Garden Friends society.

24. The book was *In Other Words* by Jhumpa Lahiri.

USDA WATERCOLOUR ARTISTS

1. This is according to General N. P. Chipman in the *Official Report of the Fruit Growers' Convention of the State of California,* vol. 10 (Sacramento: J. D. Young, 1889), p. 140.

2. Ibid.

3. Newton's seven objectives for his term as commissioner were (1) collecting, arranging and publishing statistical and other useful agricultural information; (2) introducing valuable plants and animals; (3) answering inquiries of farmers regarding agriculture; (4) testing agricultural implements; (5) conducting chemical analyses of soils, grains, fruits, plants, vegetables and manures; (6) establishing a professorship of botany and entomology; and (7) establishing an agricultural library and museum.

4. *Report of the Commissioner of Agriculture for the Year 1862* (Washington, DC: Government Printing Office, 1863), p. 17.

5. When painting apples, the watercolour artists usually showed seeds in one ovary, leaving the other empty, so as to give comprehensive knowledge of what an apple would look like with seeds and without.

6. List of federal employees from the Register of Civil, Military, and Naval Service, 1863–1959, vol. 1. From the Department of Commerce and Labor, Bureau of the Census, *Official Register of the United States, Containing a List of the Officers and Employees in the Civil, Military, and Naval Service* (Salem, OR: Oregon State Library), available online through ancestry.com.

7. Ibid.

8. The illustrators were given job titles such as clerk, modeller, botanical artist, artist and associate botanist. This information is derived from Alan E. Fusonie, "The Heritage of Original Art and Photo Imaging in USDA: Past, Present and Future," *Agricultural History*, vol. 64, no. 2 (Spring 1990): pp. 300–14.

9. From the *Washington Post,* October 20, 1905.

10. Fusonie, "The Heritage of Original Art and Photo Imaging in USDA."

11. All the USDA watercolour paintings have been digitally preserved and are available to view online at https://usdawatercolors.nal.usda.gov.

12. The artists often painted less-than-perfect specimens of apples, showing not the homogenous glossy object we are used to encountering in our grocery stores but the kinds of fruit that would be found in a small orchard or in the "wild." The apples were often lopsided or full of blemishes and spots, and a few were even rotten in places.

13. She had it constructed out of concrete to save it from fire because her family home had burned to the ground a few years earlier.

14. The collection of Ellen Schutt's apple watercolours is held at the University of California at Davis. The entire collection is now available online. See http://blogs.lib.ucdavis.edu/specol /2015/03/03/ellen-schutt-pomological-watercolors -now-online/ for more information.

15. Cherrydale Historic District, National Register of Historic Places, National Parks Service, https:// npgallery.nps.gov/nrhp/.

16. My grandfather's name was Ronald Brett. Examples of his posters can be found online at various fine art auction houses.

17. This unpublished and anonymous biography of Deborah Griscom Passmore is in the collection of her papers at the National Agricultural Library, Special Collections, Beltsville, MD. See

https://specialcollections.nal.usda.gov/speccoll/collectionsguide/passmore/124ExtBio.pdf.

18. Ibid.

19. Marianne North (1830–1890) travelled widely, painting botanical specimens that were then exhibited at Kew Gardens in England. Today, you can still see her work on display there at the Marianne North Gallery, http://www.kew.org/kew-gardens/attractions/marianne-north-gallery.

20. This work remains unpublished and is in the special collections of the National Agricultural Library in Beltsville, MD, https://www.nal.usda.gov.

21. This information also comes from the unpublished and anonymous biography at the National Agricultural Library.

22. Ibid.

23. Ibid.

24. James Marion Shull, *Rainbow Fragments: A Garden Book of the Iris* (New York: Doubleday, Doran and Co., 1931), p. 11.

25. James Marion Shull, *The Washington Peace Carillon; A Brochure Issued by Lovers of the Bells and Dedicated to Others of Their Kind* (Washington, DC: M.W. Darling, 1919).

ROBERT FROST

1. Thomas wrote five books in eight years and frequently produced fifteen book reviews per week.

2. Matthew Hollis, *Now All Roads Lead to France: The Last Years of Edward Thomas* (London: Faber & Faber, 2011), p. 338.

3. Jean Moorcroft Wilson, *Edward Thomas: From Adlestrop to Arras* (London: Bloomsbury, 2015), p. 242.

4. Matthew Spencer, ed., *Elected Friends: Robert Frost and Edward Thomas to One Another* (New York: Handsell Books, 2003), p. xviii.

5. Ibid., p. 210.

6. Ibid., p. 32.

7. Wilson, Edward Thomas: *From Adlestrop to Arras*, p. 280.

8. Spencer, *Elected Friends*, p. 136.

9. Hollis, *Now All Roads Lead to France*, p. 151.

10. Ibid., p. 327.

11. Mark Richardson, ed., *The Collected Prose of Robert Frost* (Cambridge, MA: Harvard University Press, 2007), p. 158.

12. The poem was originally written by Callimachus in 260 BC. This translation is by William Johnson Cory (1823–92), an Eton schoolmaster.

13. This has not happened before or since, although at the time we did not credit it with being unusual.

14. Joanne Page, "Bateau Channel," unpublished poem in the collection of the author.

15. Carole Thompson, "An Unforbidden Variety: The Story of Robert Frost's Apple Trees at the Stone House, Shaftsbury, Vermont" (an essay for the Robert Frost Stone House Museum in Shaftsbury, VT), http://www.frostfriends.org/apples.html.

16. Bruce Fish, Becky Fish, and Harold Bloom, *Bloom's BioCritiques: Robert Frost* (New York: Infobase Publishing, 2002), p. 46.

17. Robert Faggen, ed., *The Notebooks of Robert Frost* (Cambridge, MA: Belknap Press, 2006), p. 379.

18. John Evangelist Walsh, *Into My Own: The English Years of Robert Frost 1912–1915* (New York: Grove Weidenfeld, 1988), p. 225.

19. Undated letter from Robert Frost to Fred Abbey of Gardenside Nurseries, in the Robert Frost Collection, Rauner Special Collections Library, Dartmouth College, Hanover, NH.

20. Unsigned and undated handwritten list of apples grafted in June 1957, possibly in Robert Frost's handwriting, in the Robert Frost Collection, Rauner Special Collections Library, Dartmouth College, Hanover, NH.

21. Calhoun, *Old Southern Apples*, p. 105.

22. Letter from Frost to Fred Abbey.

23. Faggen, *Notebooks of Robert Frost*, p. 447.
24. Undated letter from Robert Frost to Ira Glackens, in the Robert Frost Collection, Rauner Special Collections Library, Dartmouth College, Hanover, NH.

THE GHOST ORCHARD

1. Eileen Woodhead, *Early Canadian Gardening: An 1827 Nursery Catalogue* (Montreal: McGill-Queen's University Press, 1998), pp. 26–27.
2. Ibid., p. 26.
3. Ibid, p. 27.
4. The architect John Nash first used the Italianate style in England in 1802. It moved to North America in the 1840s, with many examples being built along the eastern coast of the United States.
5. State Horticultural Association of Pennsylvania, *A List of Apples, Pears, Peaches, Plums and Cherries*, p. 46.
6. Henry David Thoreau, *Wild Apples* (Boston: Houghton Mifflin Company, 1923), p. 39.
7. Ibid., p. 38.
8. Wilfrid Mellers, "Modernism's Child," *New Republic,* vol. 204, no. 14 (April 8, 1991): p. 39.
9. The English cider known as scrumpy comes from this term. It's a lethally potent cider made from

small or discarded apples, and it has a stronger alcohol content than most commercially produced ciders.

A GLOSSARY OF LOST APPLES

1. Calhoun, *Old Southern Apples*, p. 178.
2. *The Horticulturist, and Journal of Rural Art and Rural Taste,* vol. 21 (New York: Geo. E. and F. W. Woodward, 1866), p. 359.
3. William Henry Ragan, *Nomenclature of the Apple: A Catalogue of the Known Varieties Referred to in American Publications from 1804 to 1904* (Washington, DC: Government Printing Office, 1905), p. 110.
4. Ibid., p. 139.
5. Calhoun, *Old Southern Apples*, p. 227.
6. Ibid., p. 229.
7. Ibid., p. 230.
8. Ibid., p. 252.
9. Ibid., p. 267.
10. Ibid., p. 269.
11. Downing and Downing, *Fruits and Fruit Trees of America*, p. 385.
12. Amos Delos Gridley, *History of the Town of Kirkland, New York* (New York: Hurd and Houghton, 1874), p. 154.

13. Calhoun, *Old Southern Apples*, p. 292.
14. Ibid., p. 293.
15. Ibid., p. 301.